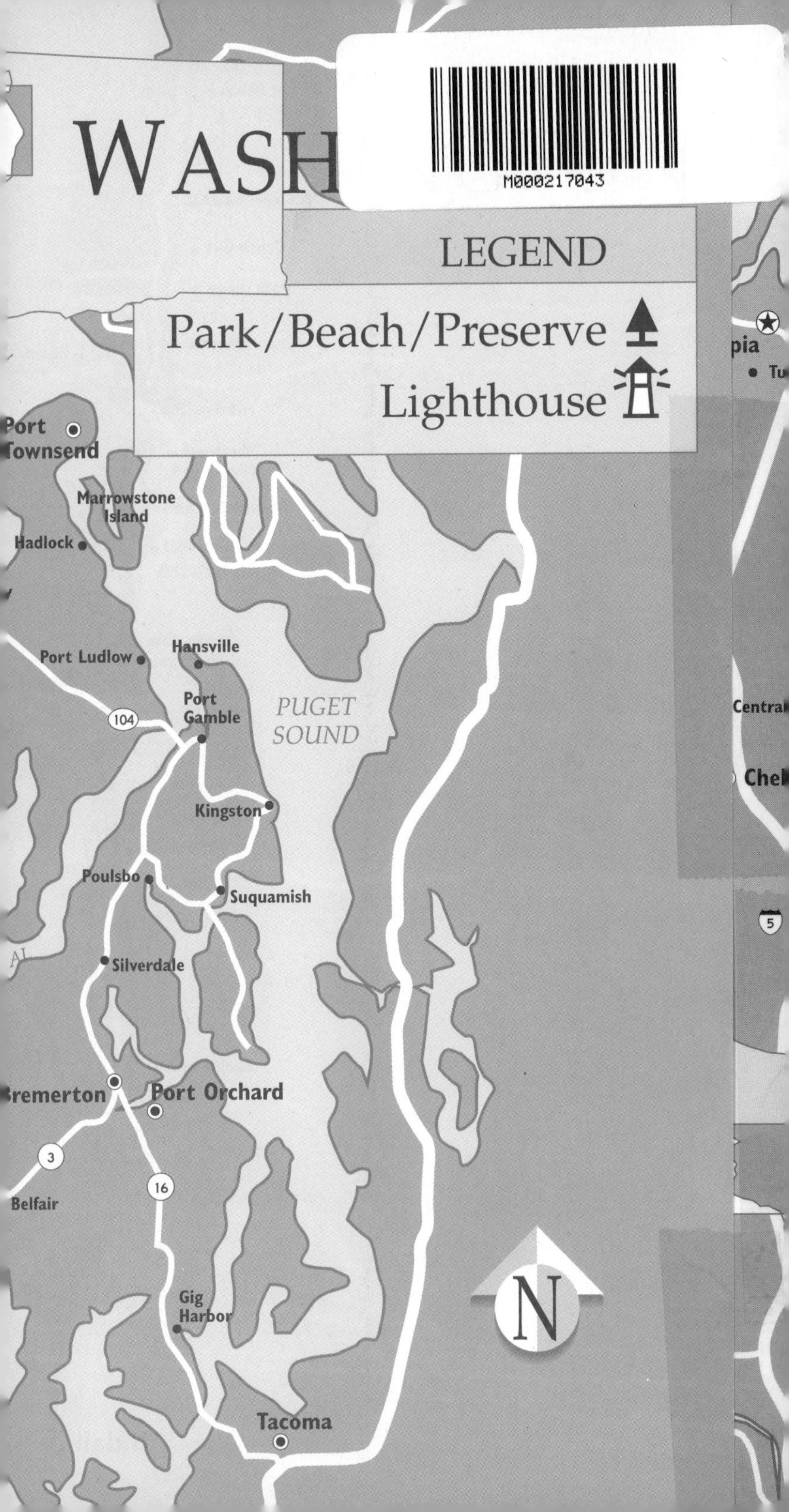
WASH
LEGEND
Park/Beach/Preserve
Lighthouse
Marrowstone Island
Hadlock
Port Ludlow
Hansville
Port Gamble
104
PUGET SOUND
Kingston
Poulsbo
Suquamish
Silverdale
Port Orchard
3
16
Belfair
Gig Harbor
Tacoma
Centra
5
N

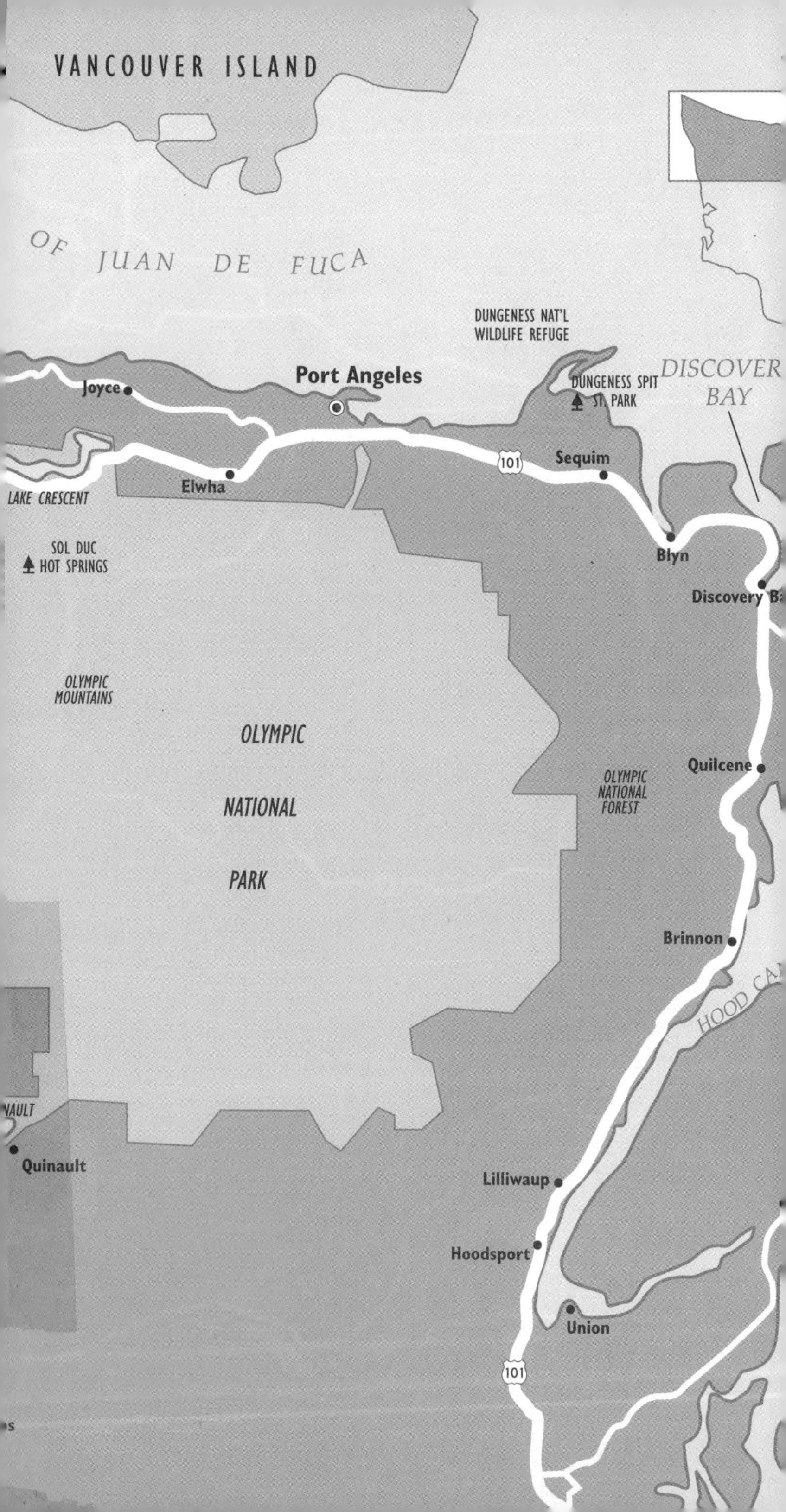

VANCOUVER ISLAND
OF JUAN DE FUCA
DUNGENESS NAT'L WILDLIFE REFUGE
DISCOVER BAY
Port Angeles
Joyce
DUNGENESS SPIT ST. PARK
101
Sequim
Elwha
LAKE CRESCENT
Blyn
SOL DUC HOT SPRINGS
Discovery B
OLYMPIC MOUNTAINS
OLYMPIC NATIONAL PARK
Quilcene
OLYMPIC NATIONAL FOREST
Brinnon
HOOD CA
NAULT
Quinault
Lilliwaup
Hoodsport
Union
101

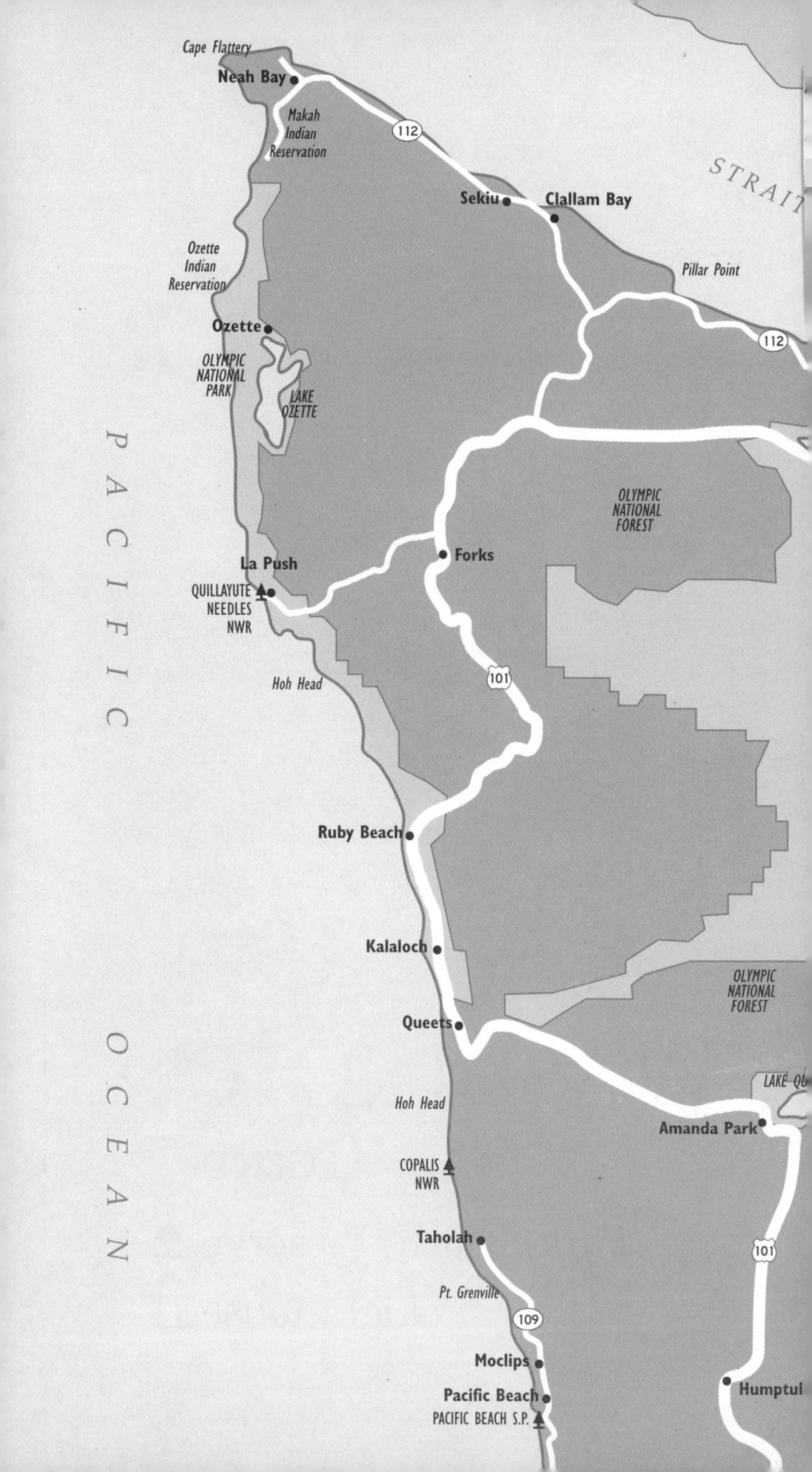
Cape Flattery
Neah Bay
Makah Indian Reservation
112
STRAIT
Sekiu
Clallam Bay
Pillar Point
Ozette Indian Reservation
Ozette
OLYMPIC NATIONAL PARK
LAKE OZETTE
112
PACIFIC OCEAN
OLYMPIC NATIONAL FOREST
Forks
La Push
QUILLAYUTE NEEDLES NWR
101
Hoh Head
Ruby Beach
Kalaloch
OLYMPIC NATIONAL FOREST
Queets
Hoh Head
Amanda Park
COPALIS NWR
Taholah
101
Pt. Grenville
109
Moclips
Pacific Beach
PACIFIC BEACH S.P.
Humptul

Tacoma
5
N
nwater
a
alis
WASHINGTON
LEGEND
Park/Beach/Preserve
Lighthouse

# OLYMPIC PENINSULA

# BEST PLACES®
## DESTINATIONS

# OLYMPIC PENINSULA

2ND EDITION

EDITED BY RACHEL BARD

SASQUATCH BOOKS
SEATTLE

Printed in the United States of America.
Published in the United States by Sasquatch Books
Distributed in Canada by Raincoast Books
Second edition

Series editor: Kate Rogers
Assistant editor: Novella Carpenter
Cover design: Nancy Gellos
Cover photo: ©Charles Mauzy/CORBIS
Foldout map: Dave Berger
Interior design adaptation and composition: Fay Bartels, Kate Basart, Millie Beard, and Dan McComb

ISSN: 1525-6561
ISBN: 1-57061-235-8

SASQUATCH BOOKS
615 Second Avenue
Seattle, WA 98104
(206)467-4300
books@SasquatchBooks.com
http://www.SasquatchBooks.com

*Special Sales*

BEST PLACES® guidebooks are available at special discounts on bulk purchases for corporate, club, or organization sales promotions, premiums, and gifts. Special editions, including personalized covers, excerpts of existing guides, and corporate imprints, can be created in large quantities for specific needs. For more information, contact your local bookseller or Special Sales, Best Places Guidebooks, 615 Second Avenue, Suite 260, Seattle, Washington 98104, 800/775-0817.

# CONTENTS

## CENTRAL COAST



## LONG BEACH PENINSULA



## HOOD CANAL

# ACKNOWLEDGMENTS

This Destination Guide could not have been produced without the invaluable assistance of the editors of and contributors to Sasquatch Books' Best Places, Budget Traveler, and Inside Out series. In particular I wish to thank Serena Lesley for her help in writing the first edition of this book, *Olympic Peninsula Best Places,* and Ron Judd for his informed insights on Olympic National Park.

*—Rachel Bard*

# ABOUT BEST PLACES GUIDEBOOKS

*Olympic Peninsula* is part of the BEST PLACES® guidebook series, which means it's written by and for locals, who enjoy getting out and exploring the region. When making our recommendations, we seek out establishments of good quality and good value, places that are independently owned, run by lively individuals, touched with local history, or sparked by fun and interesting decor. Every place listed is recommended.

BEST PLACES® guidebooks, which have been published continuously since 1975, represent one of the most respected regional travel series in the country. Each guide is written completely independently: no advertisers, no sponsors, no favors. Our reviewers know their territory, work incognito, and seek out the very best a city or region has to offer. We provide tough, candid reports and describe the true strengths, foibles, and unique characteristics of each establishment listed.

*Note: Readers are advised that the reviews in this edition are based on information available at press time and are subject to change. The editors welcome information conveyed by users of this book, as long as they have no financial connection with the establishment concerned. A report form is provided at the end of the book, and feedback is also welcome via email: books@SasquatchBooks.com.*

# HOW TO USE THIS BOOK

## ACTIVITIES

Each town throughout this area has a variety of activities and attractions from which to choose. For quick and easy reference, we've created basic symbols to represent them, with full details immediately following. Watch for these symbols:

*Arts and crafts, galleries*

*Beaches, swimming, beachcombing, water recreation*

*Bicycling*

*Boating, kayaking, other on-the-water activities*

*Entertainment: movies, theater, concerts, performing arts, events*

*Fishing (salt water and fresh)*

*Food and drinks*

*Historical sites, lighthouses*

*Kid-friendly, family activities*

*Local produce, farmers markets, farm products, organic foods*

*Parks, wilderness areas, outdoor recreation, picnics*

*Shops: clothing, books, antiques, souvenirs*

*Views, scenic driving tours, other attractions*

*Whale watching, bird watching, other wildlife viewing*

## RECOMMENDED RESTAURANTS AND LODGINGS

At the end of each town section you'll find restaurants and lodgings recommended by our BEST PLACES® editors.

***Rating System*** Establishments with stars have been rated on a scale of zero to four. Ratings are based on uniqueness, value, loyalty of local clientele, excellence of cooking, performance measured against goals, and professionalism of service.

| | |
|---|---|
| (*no stars*) | Worth knowing about, if nearby |
| ★ | A good place |
| ★★ | Some wonderful qualities |
| ★★★ | Distinguished, many outstanding features |
| ★★★★ | The very best in the region |

View Watch for this symbol throughout the book, indicating those restaurants and lodgings that feature a coastal or water view.

***Price Range*** When prices range between two categories (for example, moderate to expensive), the lower one is given. Call ahead to verify.

| | |
|---|---|
| $$$ | Expensive. Indicates a tab of more than $80 for dinner for two, including wine (but not tip), and more than $100 for one night's lodging for two. |
| $$ | Moderate. Falls between expensive and inexpensive. |
| $ | Inexpensive. Indicates a tab of less than $35 for dinner, and less than $75 for lodgings for two. |

***Email and Web Site Addresses*** With the understanding that more people are using email and the World Wide Web to access information and to plan trips, BEST PLACES® has included email and Web site addresses of establishments, where available. Please note that the World Wide Web is a fluid and evolving medium, and that Web pages are often "under construction" or, as with all time-sensitive information in a guidebook such as this, may be no longer valid.

***Checks and Credit Cards*** Most establishments that accept checks also require a major credit card for identification. Credit cards are abbreviated in this book as follows: American Express (AE); Diners Club (DC); Discover (DIS); MasterCard (MC); Visa (V).

***Directions*** Throughout the book, basic directions are provided with each restaurant and lodging. Call ahead, however, to confirm hours and location.

***Bed-and-Breakfasts*** Many B&Bs have a two-night minimum-stay requirement during the peak season, and several do not welcome children. Ask about a B&B's policies before you make your reservation.

***Smoking*** Most establishments along the Olympic Peninsula do not permit smoking inside, although some lodgings have rooms reserved for smokers. Call ahead to verify an establishment's smoking policy.

***Pets*** Most establishments do not allow pets; call ahead to verify, however, as some budget places do.

***Index*** All restaurants, lodgings, town names, and major tourist attractions are listed alphabetically at the back of the book.

***Reader Reports*** At the end of the book is a report form. We receive hundreds of reports from readers suggesting new places or agreeing or disagreeing with our assessments. They greatly help in our evaluations. We encourage you to respond.

# BAINBRIDGE ISLAND

# BAINBRIDGE ISLAND

Bainbridge Island, a 35-minute ferry ride from Seattle, is a semi-rural haven for city professionals, writers, artists, and people seeking simpler lives who don't mind a commute. For day-trippers and weekenders it offers a pleasant tour by car or bike: a dip into a world of small pastoral farms, imposing beach homes, spectacular cityscapes, agreeable waterfront parks, a number of fine restaurants, and, for those who spend the night, a choice of very congenial lodgings. For those heading for the Olympic Peninsula and its crown jewel, Olympic National Park, it's the ideal gateway, where you ease yourself away from city pressures and begin to assume the proper mindset for what's to come—a venture into one of America's last great wilderness retreats.

## WINSLOW

Ten years ago the islanders voted to become the city of Bainbridge Island, and Winslow legally ceased to exist. But it's unlikely to die out as the name of the town that greets you as you get off the ferry. Don't go barreling westward on Highway 305 without pausing here. Winslow has an increasingly interesting recreational area on Eagle Harbor where historic homes have been recycled to blend with the new construction and where the marina lends a nautical flavor. You could spend a day on Winslow Way, the town's main street, investigating a clutch of friendly, unusual, and tempting shops, galleries, and eateries. All this accessibility makes Winslow a desirable destination for foot travelers on the ferry. For orientation, stop at the Chamber of Commerce on the right-hand corner as you enter town (509 Winslow Way; 206/842-3700). Pick up an island map and a Downtown Walkabout map and guide, and you're set.

***A pleasant approach to Winslow is the five-minute stroll along the footpath that runs from the ferry through Waterfront Park along the shore, ending at Bainbridge Island Common, with benches and picnic tables along the way. Then head up to Winslow Way. Bay Hay and Feed (10355 NE Valley Road; 206/842-2813) is an old-fashioned country store where folks come to stock up on garden equipment, clothing, food—to say nothing of hay and feed—and to catch up on the gossip. A coffee shop with outdoor seating serves goodies from Bainbridge Bakers.***

## ACTIVITIES

***Coffee Stops.*** At the foot of Madison Avenue S, Pegasus Coffee House and Gallery (206/842-3113) is a relaxed hangout where conversation and lattes flow. Up the hill at Winslow Green, the shopping crescent on the southwest corner of Winslow Way and Madison, Bainbridge Bakers (206/842-1822) is famous for its pastries and breads; sit outside and feel like an islander.

## GETTING TO BAINBRIDGE

***The easiest access from the Seattle area is by Washington State Ferries; ferries sail frequently from Seattle's Colman Dock (Pier 2, Alaskan Way and Marion Street). For schedules and information, call 888/808-7977 (Washington only) or 206/464-6400; or consult the web page, www.wsdot.wa.gov/ferries/. Get in line early, especially during commuter hours and on summer weekends. Or you could arrive by the back door: drive through Tacoma, across the Narrows Bridge, and up the Kitsap Peninsula to Poulsbo, where you follow Highway 305 east and cross the Agate Pass Bridge to Bainbridge.***

***Bainbridge has its share of wacky festivals. Come in May for the Scotch Broom Parade, when the broom-bedecked residents promenade down Winslow Way and the main feature is a tiddlywinks contest.***

***Literary Lights.*** The island is famed as a home or hideout for writers, and you can get a list of about 100 resident authors at Eagle Harbor Book Co. (157 Winslow Way E; 206/842-5332). It's sprinkled with familiar names—David Guterson, Ann Lovejoy, Jack Olsen—and others whose books could give you a leg up on getting to know the island. The store is fully stocked with off-island books too, and the staff brims with helpfulness.

***The Arts Scene.*** Bainbridge Arts and Crafts (151 Winslow Way; 206/842-3132), is a nonprofit showcase for local and regional artists; profits go to arts education in the schools. Exhibits change monthly and you'll always find choice works in every medium for sale, displayed as handsomely as in a museum. While there, pick up a copy of the quarterly *Arts News* to find out what the current cultural scene offers.

***Paddle the Bay.*** Rent a canoe or kayak and get guidance from Bainbridge Island Boat Rentals, 265 Winslow Way; 206/842-9229. The company has an outpost down on the harbor at Waterfront Park, too.

***Go to the Flicks.*** The good old Tudor-style Lynnwood Theater (206/842-3080), until 1999 the island's only motion picture theater, is out at Lynnwood Center, a few miles south of Winslow on Lynnwood Center Road; the velvet curtain creaks as it rolls back, and the popcorn's first-rate. Make a festive evening of it, with dinner at Ruby's next door (see Restaurants, below).

***Bloedel Reserve.*** On the northeast shore of Bainbridge, accessible from Highway 305, this tranquil 150-acre expanse of gardens, meadows, woodlands, streams, and ponds merits at least two hours of your time on the island. It's transfixing from the moment you begin your walk through a bucolic meadow. You will come upon gardens both formally English and serenely Japanese; a lush rhododendron glen; a moss garden in the heart of a forest, carpeted with velvety green; and a marsh dedicated to birds. It's worth repeat visits as the seasons change. No food service, no picnicking. Open Wednesday through Sunday, by reservation only (call well in advance); $6 admission, $4 for seniors; 7571 NE Dolphin Drive, Bainbridge Island; 206/842-7631.

***Fay-Bainbridge State Park.*** For such a large island, there's precious little public waterfront. So be grateful for a couple of state parks where you may walk the beach, picnic, doze on a log, skip rocks, launch a boat, hunt for agates—all those good beachy things. Fay-Bainbridge State Park, on the north end, is one of the best things about Bainbridge. It has a 1,400-foot smooth sandy beach, picnicking spots nearby, and an eye-popping view of the Seattle skyline; also 36 tightly spaced campsites. Expect plenty of company here on nice summer days. Take the Day Road turnoff east from Highway 305 and follow signs.

***Maybe there should have been, but there never was a Fay Bainbridge. The Fay in the park's hyphenated name comes from Temple S. Fay, the original property owner.***

***Fort Ward State Park.*** At the island's southern end, larger Fort Ward State Park has a beach that is not quite so accessible but it is three times as long and far less crowded. Look for shorebirds—there's a bird blind at each end of the beach. Offshore, Orchard Rocks attracts scuba divers to anemone-filled grottoes; extreme caution is advised. The park also has an upland, forested area with trails; a loop of beach and woods is about 2 miles. Added attractions: a couple of mossy old gun batteries dating from before World War I, placed here to protect the naval shipyard at Bremerton. There's no camping, but there is kayak access; this is a stop on the Cascadia Water Trail.

Fort Ward is reached from the northwest (end of Pleasant Beach Road) or from the south (by Fort Ward Hill Road); get a map at the tourist office.

***Home-Grown Wines.*** Bainbridge Island Winery (206/842-WINE), just a few strides up the road from the ferry, is

***Plan your Bainbridge visit to include a summertime Wednesday evening, and take in a free concert in Waterfront Park.***

a small, family-owned winery, with its own vineyards and berry fields. Besides its popular strawberry and raspberry dessert wines, it produces a well-regarded pinot noir and Müller-Thurgau, among other varieties. Come and taste, visit the wine museum, have a picnic, shop for antiques. Open afternoons, Wednesday through Sunday.

***Bainbridge Gardens.*** This enchanting 7-acre spread is far more than a nursery, though it's that too: whatever your heart's desire in things botanical, it's here somewhere along the maze of walks, greenhouses, arbors, and sheds. Also find fountains and statuary, ceramic pots and pruning shears, even a plant pharmacy, where you get expert advice on your plants' ailments. Plan to spend an hour or so, whether you have a shopping list or not, just wandering; include a side trip across the little bridge to the nature trail in the forest. The garden's appeal grows when you know its history: begun in 1908 by Zenhichi Harui, it was abandoned when he was interned during WW II, then restored and amplified by his son Junkoh Harui. 9415 Miller Road NE; 206/842-5888; open daily.

***Time Out for Lunch.*** The New Rose Cafe, tucked away at one end of Bainbridge Gardens, is small, unpretentious, and welcoming to passers-through as well as to garden shoppers. Eat under cover or al fresco, in the shade of a tall, bonsai-like red pine, grown by the elder Mr. Harui from seeds he brought from Japan nearly a century ago. The cafe serves espresso, snacks, salads, soups, and lunch entrees, as well as beer and wine, every day; 206/842-4438.

***Biking the Island.*** Bring your bike on the ferry (it costs only 60 cents more than passenger fare) and see the island with pedal power. Map your route to get yourself off traffic-heavy Highway 305 as quickly as possible and head for the back roads. Fay-Bainbridge State Park is a good destination, about 7 miles from the ferry terminal. Or do the whole hilly 30-mile Bainbridge Loop: start on Ferncliff, heading north, at the ferry terminal and work your way counterclockwise around the island (follow the signs). Bikes may be rented at B.I. Cycle Shop, 162 Bjune Drive (below Winslow Way), PO Box 10102, Bainbridge Island; 206/842-6413.

**Chilly Hilly.** Hardy bikers from all over Puget Sound start the season with the Chilly Hilly, a February event that the Cascade Bicycle Club promotes as a warm-up to the Seattle-Portland ride. Part of the route approximates the 30-mile Bainbridge Loop. This is one of the few biking routes in Kitsap County with a stretch right along the shore, on Point White Road at the island's south end. Not a biker? Bundle up and stand by the road to cheer.

## RESTAURANTS

### BISTRO PLEASANT BEACH ★★

Hussein and Laura Ramadan closed their white-linen place in an old Tudor mansion on Bainbridge Island's southwest corner, built a smart new restaurant on the edge of downtown Winslow, dumped the white linen, and became the island's most chic spot the moment they opened. Though the bistro seats as many as 160 when the weather's fair (60 on the main floor, 40 on the mezzanine level, and another 60 on the broad patio), when dinnertime rolls around it fills to the gills. Then it's kiss-kiss, wave-wave, and everyone settles down to Mediterranean-inflected, local-ingredient food: baked brie with walnuts, five-onion bisque, Greek-accent pasta, wood-oven-fired pizza, curried lamb stew, and grilled Atlantic salmon from Bainbridge's fish farm. *241 Winslow Wy W, Bainbridge Island; ½ block west of Madison; 206/842-4347; $$; AE, MC, V; local checks only; lunch Tues–Fri, dinner Tues–Sun, brunch Sat–Sun; beer and wine.* ♿

### CAFE NOLA ★★

Imagine holding a bowl of café au lait in both hands and having a heart-to-heart with a friend. Thanks to sisters Melinda Lucas and Mary Bugarin, you needn't fly to France for the experience. After successful California careers they came to Bainbridge and established this elegant French Provençal cafe complete with a lavender-lined patio for good-weather idling. Melinda (a former pastry chef at L.A.'s Spago) is responsible for the scrumptious pastries, beautiful desserts, and exceptional breads. Mary (a former San Francisco caterer) prepares the extraordinary soups, salads, sandwiches, pastas, and pizzas. Breakfast features the freshest eggs imaginable, along with perfect fruits for topping granola and oatmeal. Heavenly Hots (tender sour-cream pancakes) with huckleberry compote mark Sundays as special. Café Nola keeps many small island farmers busy growing organic produce—and gathering organic eggs—to satisfy the cafe's exacting standards. Monthly wine dinners give the sisters opportunities to prepare the likes of open-face ravioli of seared wild salmon with white-corn sauce, grilled pea vines, and roasted pepper–infused oil. *101 Winslow Way, Bainbridge Island; 206/842-3822; $–$$; MC, V; checks OK; breakfast, lunch Tues–Sun; beer and wine.*

## FOUR SWALLOWS

Michael Sharp and chef Geraldine Ferraro preside over this restaurant and are totally serious about transforming fresh Northwest ingredients into fine cuisine with an Italian twist. One—or two, or three—could partake of the antipasto and go home perfectly happy; its dozen offerings could include tapenade, marinated mushrooms, crisp crunchy fennel strips and green beans, basil-dusted goat cheese, roasted beets, and other delicacies depending on the season. The Manila clams in the clam linguini are tiny and tender; cioppino fanciers will fancy the *brodetto,* with generous portions of fish and shellfish. Besides pizzas and pastas, there are one or two beef and chicken choices among the entrees. Dessert (made right here) could be an intensely flavored fruit sorbet, or perhaps the ultimate indulgence: a dense, smooth cube of chocolate pâté, flanked by pools of crème Anglaise and raspberry *coulis.* Besides an impressive list of wines by the bottle, there's a rotating selection of respectable wines by the glass. *481 Madison Ave, Bainbridge Island; 1 block west of Winslow Way on Madison; 206/842-3397; $$; AE, MC, V; local checks only; dinner Tues–Sat; beer and wine.*

## HARBOUR PUBLIC HOUSE

This friendly pub on Bainbridge's Eagle Harbor, near the marina, is an easy stroll from the ferry dock. Its core is one of Winslow's historic 19th-century homes, but today it's pure pub—if brighter and airier than some. In winter it is cozy and amber-lit; in summer, sunlight slants through loft windows and onto the waterside deck. There's a connoisseur's selection of lagers and ales along with a broad list of wines, ports, and sherries. And there's an enlightened menu of food, from traditional pub fare to pasta. *231 Parfitt Way SW, Bainbridge Island; 206/842-0969; $; AE, MC, V; local checks only; lunch and dinner every day; beer and wine.*

## RUBY'S ON BAINBRIDGE ★★

Maura and Aaron Crisp turned this location next door to the island's pioneer movie theater into a minidestination restaurant. It's a steamy, garlicky little place a hobbit might love—just casual enough for the locals, just sumptuous enough for weekend guests and day-trippers. The menu changes often, but you'll encounter entrees such as fettuccine tossed with wild mushrooms, swordfish dressed in soy and ginger, and pork tenderloin with a raspberry reduction. *4569 Lynnwood Center Rd, Bainbridge Island; 206/780-9303; follow Wyatt Way, Bucklin Hill Rd, Lynnwood Center Rd to Lynnwood Center; $$; MC, V; checks OK; lunch Tues–Sun, dinner every day, brunch Sat–Sun; beer and wine.*

## SAWATDY THAI CUISINE ★★

Bainbridge Islanders don't need to ferry over to the Big City for a taste of Thailand: they're convinced that some of the best Thai food in the Seattle area can be found right here. The place runs like clockwork, and you can rest assured that every fragrant dish, from the eggplant lover's platter to the coriander beef with sticky rice, is well executed and every customer well cared for. Hold your decision until you've had a chance to talk to your server, who can give you the inside scoop on what dish "Mom" is cooking best that night. Reservations are a good idea. *8770 Fletcher Bay Rd, Bainbridge Island; take Hwy 305, turn west on High School Rd, then north on Fletcher Bay Rd to Island Center; 206/780-2429; $; MC, V; checks OK; lunch Mon–Fri, dinner every day; beer and wine.*

## STREAMLINER DINER

First pit stop up from the ferry dock, this crowded little diner changes owners about every three years. Locals don't seem to mind. They sit around swilling coffee (no espresso here!) for hours on end, chasing morning into afternoon. The lackadaisical vibes generated by relaxed islanders make the Streamliner a ferry-ride destination for mainlanders. The grub mostly remains within diner boundaries, with a few effete touches like tofu scramble, quiche, and Cajun mayo on the meat-loaf sandwich. The signature dish, potatoes deluxe, rises above kitchen-sink cooking through the inclusion of fresh spinach. The fried-egg-and-bacon sandwich earns local renown. Don't miss a big slice of fruit pie baked by a local pastry wizard. But resist the "Warm-'er-up?" temptation; nuking this flaky crust into a soggy mass ought to be a gross misdemeanor. *397 Winslow Way, Bainbridge Island; 206/842-8595; $; no credit cards; checks OK; breakfast every day, lunch Mon–Sat; no alcohol.* ♿

## LODGINGS

### THE BUCHANAN INN ★

Innkeepers Ron and Judy Gibbs have added a touch of sophistication to this beautifully renovated Odd Fellows Hall built in 1912. Located in one of Bainbridge Island's most picturesque neighborhoods, the garden-surrounded B&B boasts high-ceilinged rooms so spacious the Odd Fellows would be comfortable convening here today. The four suites have separate sitting rooms, king- or queen-size beds, and refrigerators stocked with complimentary beverages. Two suites have antique gas fireplaces. If you prefer to leave your jammies on during the breakfast hour you can request a continental breakfast basket be brought to your room. (If you're the more sociable type, a complete gourmet breakfast is served in the formal dining room.) Just a few minutes away are Fort Ward State Park and the beach—and it's only a few steps to the rustic cottage where a bubbling hot tub awaits. Pets and children under 16 are not allowed unless the entire inn is reserved. *8494 NE Odd Fellows Rd, Bainbridge Island; 4 miles from Winslow off Blakely Ave; 800/598-3926 or 206/780-9258; jgibbs@buchananinn.com; www.buchananinn.com; $$–$$$; AE, DIS, MC, V; checks OK.*

# KITSAP PENINSULA

# KITSAP PENINSULA

Geographically, it's an in-between kind of place: across the sound to the east lies urban, animated Seattle and the Interstate 5 corridor; to the west across Hood Canal, the mostly wild Olympic Peninsula extends all the way to the Pacific Ocean. The Kitsap Peninsula has forged a winning personality that blends moderate degrees of civilization and near-wilderness, with the plus of easy access. You'll find small towns with all the amenities, a jumbo shopping center, sophisticated restaurants, and luxurious lodgings. You'll also find, along 236 miles of shoreline, a dozen parks that offer outdoor experiences from mild to wild: beach walking, kayaking, scuba diving, camping, bird-watching, sitting on a log. Up in the timbered hills, many a lakeside park is a place for fishing and solitude. Were it not for Uncle Sam, there would be more public beach access, but a lot of shoreline has been gobbled up by a trio of impressive and economy-boosting military complexes: the Puget Sound Naval Shipyard in Bremerton, the Naval Undersea Warfare Center in Keyport, and the Bangor Naval Submarine Base.

## ACTIVITIES

***Cycling Kitsap.*** Kitsap's country roads don't abound in bike lanes or wide shoulders, but with the help of a map you'll be able to avoid the riskier routes. Good idea: Let someone else do the planning and come for one of the annual events.

***For a bargain cruise to the Kitsap Peninsula, take the ferry from Fauntleroy in West Seattle, stop off for a visit on Vashon Island, then continue via the Vashon-Southworth ferry; there's no fee when you leave Vashon.***

### VISITORS' INFORMATION

***Most towns on the peninsula have tourist information centers: in Port Orchard, at 839 Bay St; 800/982-8139 or 360/876-3505; Bremerton, 301 Pacific or PO Box 229; 360/479-3579; Silverdale, PO Box 1218; 360/692-6800; Poulsbo, PO Box 1063; 360/779-4848; Kingston, PO Box 78; 360/297-3813. A visit to the county-wide visitor bureau in historic Port Gamble is highly recommended. It's a central source of information about the whole Kitsap Peninsula, in one of the town's charming old houses. Kitsap Peninsula Visitor & Convention Bureau, 2 Rainier, PO Box 270, Port Gamble; 800/416-5615 or 360/297-8200; info@visitkitsap.com; www.visitkitsap.com.***

## GETTING TO KITSAP PENINSULA

***By ferry you have several choices. For the longest (one hour) and most scenic ride, take the Seattle-Bremerton route, which wends its way across the Sound, skirts southern Bainbridge Island, and threads its way through fjordlike Rich Passage. Or take the Seattle-Bainbridge route and drive west from Bainbridge across the Agate Pass Bridge; or Seattle-Southworth from Fauntleroy, or Edmonds-Kingston. Farther south, you can take a spectacular drive over the Tacoma Narrows Bridge or, from Olympia, go west to Shelton and then follow Highway 3 north. For ferry information call 888/808-7977 (Washington only) or 206/464-6400; or access the web page, www.wsdot.wa.gov/ferries/. Kitsap Transit, 360/373-BUSS, meets ferries at Southworth, Bremerton, and Winslow on Bainbridge Island, and Kingston, and covers Kitsap Peninsula from Port Orchard to Hansville; it also connects with Jefferson Transit, which serves Port Townsend.***

Besides the Chilly Hilly (see Bainbridge Island chapter), there's the Trident Triple at the Naval Submarine Base in Bangor; all routes include a tour of the base and views of its submarine pier. The West Sound Cycle Club usually has a couple of organized events a year, around Port Orchard and Bremerton; www.hollynewsnet.org/WSCC. Out at Tahuya south of Belfair, there are miles of trails through the forest. Contact the Department of Natural Resources for a Tahuya map ($2): PO Box 68, Enumclaw, WA 98022. The Kitsap Visitor Bureau web page has directions for North Kitsap and South Kitsap tours: www.visitkitsap.com, or call them at 800/416-5615. For supplies and rentals, consult Mount Constance Mountain Shoppe in Bremerton, 360/377-0668; Silverdale Cyclery, 360/692-5508; Missing Link in Poulsbo, 360/697-2453; or Olympic Outdoor Center in Poulsbo, 360/697-6095.

***Gardeners Alert.*** For how-to tips or just for looking, take a tour of Kitsap's enchanting gardens and nurseries. The Visitor Bureau has a partial list on the web site, www.visitkitsap.

com, or a more complete printed list of a score of spots you may visit, from herb farms to a bonsai gallery; 800/416-5615.

## PORT ORCHARD

Port Orchard seems relaxed compared with Bremerton, the serious port just across Sinclair Inlet. But Port Orchard, a mere 15 minutes from the Southworth ferry terminal via a pleasant shoreside drive, is very serious about dressing up its downtown waterfront. Along arcaded Bay Street, the main drag, cafes, taverns, delis, and antique emporiums flourish and shoppers meander, protected from the rain. Port Orchard claims the title of antique capital of the Kitsap Peninsula.

***Port Orchard loves vintage boats and cars and you're invited to ogle them when they come to town. Every July Chris-Craft boaters rendezvous in their lovingly restored vessels at the Port Orchard Marina for a couple of days of camaraderie; and in August the Cruz happens—owners of vintage cars assemble on the waterfront to show off their polished Mustangs and Thunderbirds.***

## ACTIVITIES

***Shops.*** One of the first and the most rewarding of Port Orchard's antique malls is Olde Central (801 Bay Street; 360/895-1902), in the former Central Hotel. Its sprawling space accommodates some 70 shops. If antiques aren't your thing, try Sidney Galleries (Port Orchard was once called Sidney), where 60 shopkeepers have banded together to offer a bewildering display of gifts and curiosities (702 Bay Street; 360/876-4622).

***Sidney Gallery and Museum.*** An enterprise of the Sidney Museum and Arts Association, Sidney Gallery shows and sells fine art in a restored historic building two blocks uphill from Bay Street (202 Sidney Street; 360/876-3693). Shows change monthly. Ascend the creaky stairs to the small historical museum, with its life-size reproductions of a 1909 schoolroom (complete with a shirtwaisted teacher and her students), and a period grocery store featuring shelves of vintage products. All of this is within easy walking distance of the marina and the three-block-long waterfront park.

***Fresh from the Market.*** Port Orchard Farmers Market takes place every Saturday, from the end of April through October, along the town's waterfront park. Wares are displayed under gaily colored canopies, and range from pottery to scones and fresh basil to Hood Canal oysters and clams. The pavilion at the east end of the park doubles as bandstand and picnic shelter.

*Myhre's Restaurant (737 Bay Street; 360/876-4634) in Port Orchard holds the record for longest continuous restaurant operation in Kitsap County: since 1927. Old photos on the walls show the town in days of yore and you can still get an old-fashioned milk shake. To reenter the 21st century, go upstairs to the Terrace Room and watch all the naval goings-on in Sinclair Inlet.*

***Hello Dollies!*** Springhouse Dolls and Gifts (1130 Bethel Avenue; 360/876-5695), a five-minute drive from downtown Port Orchard, boasts the largest collection of modern dolls in the Northwest. You may enjoy breakfast, lunch, or afternoon tea Sunday through Tuesday, dinner Wednesday through Saturday, in the pretty, frilly Victorian Rose Tearoom, or out on the terrace with a calming view of lawn, gardens, and woods. Wednesdays and Saturdays at 3pm, by reservation, high tea is served. Order the pricier Victorian High Tea and you get a floral china teacup to take home. But you may simply order an espresso, a pot of tea, and a scone anytime. This place won't let you go away hungry; a new ice cream shop in the blue Victorian addition across the parking lot will fill that last chink in your tummy. As for the dolls and teddy bears, they're almost as irresistible as the Victorian Rose bread pudding with rose-cinnamon sauce.

***Minicruise.*** A privately owned foot-ferry runs every half hour, year-round, between downtown Bremerton and Port Orchard (Horluck Transportation Company, 360/876-2300). The 15-minute cruise is no-frills; the little boats have no refreshment counter or upholstered seats. It costs $1.50 for adults, 75 cents for children 6 to 11, and children 5 and under are free. On weekends between April and October the *Carlisle II,* a 75-year-old double-decker ferry dating from the days of the famed Mosquito Fleet, makes the run, and the trip is free.

***Fore!*** Golfers have a half dozen or more choices on the Kitsap Peninsula, including the Trophy Lake Golf and Casting Club southwest of Port Orchard, which welcomes both golfers and fishermen in a resortlike atmosphere. 3900 SW Lake Flora Road; 360/874-8337.

***Manchester State Park.*** The sprawling, lushly forested park lies 6 miles east of Port Orchard off Beach Drive, the road to the Southworth ferry; the park is 4 miles from the turnoff. Once a fort, it still preserves a huge torpedo warehouse, now a picnic shelter. There are trails along the shore, and rocks that make good fishing platforms. The beach isn't great for swimming, but divers love it. Campers will find 53 sites (no reservations).

***Not-So-Secret Gardens.*** On the shores of Sinclair Inlet, tranquil Elandan Gardens (3050 W State Highway 16, Port Orchard; 360/373-8260) is neither garden nor nursery—it's a 5-acre, open-air gallery of bonsai accompanied by sculpture, skeletal driftwood spires and logs, and native trees and shrubs. Dan Robinson, who created this masterpiece with his wife, Diane, and their extended family, has been devoted to bonsai art for 35 years. Some of his tiny, elegantly shaped junipers were alive when King Alfred reigned, more than 1,000 years ago. The gift shop is like a gallery too, with choice antiques and furnishings and works of art from around the world. Have an espresso and consider buying your own miniature tree. The gardens, open Tuesday through Sunday, are in Gorst, between Port Orchard and Bremerton, just beyond milepost 28 on Highway 16, coming from Port Orchard. If eastbound, look for the U-turn sign on the road to Port Orchard and turn around; or, more safely, continue on Highway 16 past Gorst, take the Tremont exit, go under the freeway and return.

***Jive with Your Java.*** Rewind Music & Coffee Co. (639 Bay Street; 360/876-9442) features espresso, ice cream, pastries, candy, and CDs. Listening posts with earphones line one wall of the funky little hangout, and customers are welcome to play tapes and CDs from the shop's collection (they're also for sale).

## RESTAURANTS

### TWETEN'S LIGHTHOUSE ★

Port Orchard's new City Hall has a taller tower, but the pseudo-lighthouse that tops Tweten's has been a Port Orchard landmark longer—since 1983. As the city's only restaurant squarely on the water, it predictably specializes in seafood. Longtime chef Drew Leger insists on the freshest (from Johnny's in Tacoma) and introduces exotic influences—Asian, Mediterranean, and Hispanic. The cedar plank–roasted salmon is accompanied by a dab of sweet-and-sour cucumber that gives a wake-up call to your taste buds. The Dungeness crab quesadilla is generously filled with crab and isn't overloaded with shredded lettuce; with the accompanying sour cream, zingy salsa, and bowl of fresh fruit, it's lunch enough for anyone. Service is quick and attentive, and every table, whether inside the big two-level restaurant or out on the deck, gets a view of Bremerton and its naval might across the bay, and the snowcapped Olympics to the west. *429 Bay St, Port Orchard; on the left as you enter town from the west; 360/876-8464; $$; AE, MC, V; checks OK; lunch and dinner every day; full bar.*

## LODGINGS

### REFLECTIONS BED AND BREAKFAST INN ★★

This sprawling B&B deserves all the superlatives that have been applied to it. It's set on a hillside overlooking Sinclair Inlet, with the snowy peaks of the Olympic Mountains in the background. Former New Englanders Jim and Cathy Hall extend warm hospitality to their guests, complete with a hearty breakfast of regional American dishes that everyone plans the night before. The Halls furnish the four guest rooms with family antiques, including heirloom quilts. The largest room, often used by honeymooners, has a private porch and Jacuzzi tub. The well-tended grounds include a hot tub, a gazebo, and a multitude of birds eating and preening at various feeders. *3878 Reflections Lane E, Port Orchard; east of Port Orchard off Beach Dr; 360/871-5582; jimreflect@hurricane.net; www.portorchard.com/reflections; $$; MC, V; checks OK.*

# BREMERTON

A few years ago *Money Magazine* named Bremerton, the hundred-year-old navy town on Sinclair Inlet, as America's most liveable city. Its residential areas are tidy, its cultural offerings are generous, and it's only a 40-minute cruise from the urban attractions of Seattle. For travelers, it makes a good day trip or stopover on the way to the rest of Kitsap or to the Olympic Peninsula. Bremerton has had some ups and downs, with its shifting populations of sailors and their families and its retail core that thrives or fades as vessels come or go in the shipyard. But the ghostly mothballed fleet in the harbor has become a prime tourist attraction, the art scene is thriving, and there's plenty of activity on the waterfront.

A stroll along the broad boardwalk that runs north from the ferry terminal is exhilarating. Sinclair Inlet is alive with vessels to-ing and fro-ing between Bremerton and ports near and far; Seattle ferries chug in and out; flags snap in the breeze; and benches, picnic tables, and sculptures dot the walkway.

***It was in Bremerton—and there's a plaque at Fourth and Pacific to prove it—that a spectator shouted at the campaigning Harry Truman, "Give 'em Hell, Harry!"—the words that became the slogan that may have helped Truman to his 1948 victory.***

## ACTIVITIES

***Tour a Historic Ship.*** At the north end of the boardwalk, get your ticket at the Ship's Store gift shop and visit the destroyer USS *Turner Joy,* famed for its role at the Gulf of Tonkin off Vietnam, winning nine battle stars during the conflict. The ship is open for self-guided tours, from boiler room to bridge; also on board is a replica of a dismal prisoner-of-war cell from the infamous Hoa Lo Prison (the "Hanoi Hilton"). Tour daily in summer, Thursday to Monday in winter; $7 adults, $6 seniors, and $5 children; 360/792-2457.

***Harbor Cruises.*** Also at the Ship's Store shop, get a ticket for a 45-minute narrated voyage with Kitsap Harbor Tours (360/792-2457) to view naval ships in port and the mothball fleet. Your little boat sails past gunmetal-gray giants: aircraft carriers, battleships, cruisers, even nuclear subs. If you're lucky the supercarrier USS *Carl Vinson*—homeported here—will be on view; with a crew of 3,000, it's one of the world's largest warships.

***Amy Burnett Fine Art Gallery.*** Occupying the Fourth and Pacific Building (look for "Galleries of West Sound" on the outside), this spacious gallery (402 Pacific, a couple of blocks up from the waterfront; 360/373-3187) displays works by Burnett and other contemporary and Northwest Coast artists.

***To see the original of Amy Burnett's famous painting of Chief Sealth, visit the Suquamish Museum in Suquamish.***

***A Showcase of Naval History.*** You don't have to be a fan of Horatio Hornblower or Patrick O'Brian to get a kick out of the Bremerton Naval Museum (a short block up from the boardwalk, at 130 Washington Street; 360/479-7447). With its displays recalling swashbuckling days of sailing vessels and its intricately detailed ship models, such as the 15-foot-long aircraft carrier *Admiral Nimitz,* it fascinates landlubbers and seafarers alike. Examine ships in bottles, ships' bells, spyglasses, capstans, and more nautical gear than you could shake a belaying pin at. And it's free. Open daily in summer, daily except Monday in winter.

*Retired Navy men gravitate to the Bremerton waterfront to look at the old ships and reminisce. "We get a lot of Navy guys' reunions," says Dave Gudgell, captain with Kitsap Harbor Tours. "I took a bunch out on a tour to see their old subtender, the* Sperry, *moored in the bay. Some of them looked at that relic with tears in their eyes."*

***Rest Stop.*** Perch for a bit in the Fraiche Cup, a calm and comfortable coffee house, with reading matter on the tables and croissants to go with your coffee, a couple of doors from the Naval Museum.

***Tour to Tillicum.*** Tillicum Village on Blake Island, midway between Seattle and the Kitsap Peninsula, offers a popular Native American experience, including a salmon dinner in the longhouse and a traditional stage show by the Tillicum Village Dancers; 360/731-0770. Call Kitsap Harbor Tours, 360/377-8924, for information on their package that includes a 45-minute cruise to Blake Island and back, and dinner; leaving from the Bremerton Boardwalk.

***The Admirable New Admiral.*** Check out the offerings at Bremerton's historic Admiral Theatre, 5th and Pacific; 360/373-6743. It's been beautifully restored to its Art Moderne glory and is the venue for all kinds of entertainments: the Seattle Symphony comes over, puppets perform, and live music across the spectrum is presented. Sometimes there's cabaret dinner theater.

***Bangor Submarine Base.*** Across Kitsap Peninsula, Bangor occupies 7,000 securely fenced acres on Hood Canal. This is home port for the huge Trident nuclear submarines, each one as long as the Space Needle is tall but far more mobile. From the shores or from Hood Canal Bridge you may sometimes see one of these steely black leviathans sliding purposefully through the water. Boaters are warned to keep their distance. Tours of the base are available on a limited, prescheduled basis (no drop-ins; all applicants are screened). For information about tours, call the base, 360/396-5003.

## RESTAURANTS

### BOAT SHED ☆

This casual seafood restaurant overhanging the Port Washington Narrows is aptly named. Rough wood panels the walls inside and out, and a fish tank serves as decor. Ducks paddle along the shore while boats of every size pass by. Whenever possible, hit the deck and enjoy a pint of ale, a gigantic serving of tangled Cajun onion strings, and a cup of rich clam chowder, or try the knockwurst piled with red onions and cheese on sourdough. Tuna coated with sesame seeds might come topped with a pat of wasabe butter; lime enlivens the Dungeness crab cakes. Even most of the pasta dishes showcase the bounty of the local waters. *101 Shore Dr, Bremerton; east side of Manette Bridge, on the water; 360/377-2600; $; MC, V; local checks only; lunch, dinner every day, brunch Sun; full bar.* ♿

## SEABECK

There isn't much more to Seabeck, west of Bremerton, than a marina, a pizzeria, a post office, a small grocery, and an enviable location on Hood Canal. Once it was a major lumber town, bigger than Seattle in the 1860s. The mill burned down long ago, but the mill pond is now the lagoon that fronts the Seabeck Conference Center, a rustic retreat that may be rented by nonprofit groups; call 360/830-5010.

## ACTIVITIES

***The Park with the Million-Dollar View.*** Scenic Beach State Park, west of Seabeck, is sheltered by massive evergreens and has a pebbly beach, good fishing from the shore, and a breathtaking view straight across the canal to the Olympics. You need to reserve for camping; 360/830-5079.

***Drama in the Woods.*** The Mountaineer Playhouse, on the Bremerton-Seabeck road, is the state's oldest theater, with performances every summer in a natural amphitheater and with seating carved out of the hillside (bring a cushion). Call the Mountaineers, 206/284-6310, for information and reservations.

## LODGINGS

### WILLCOX HOUSE ★★★

Colonel Julian Willcox and his wife, Constance, once played hosts to such famous guests as Clark Gable at this copper-roofed, art deco, 10,000-square-foot manse on Hood Canal. Oak parquet floors, walnut-paneled walls, and a mammoth copper-framed marble fireplace grace the enormous front rooms. Also on this floor are the Pub (which doubles as a small video theater), a game room, and a clubby library where you can look out over the canal and the impressive gardens. Each of the five guest rooms has a view of the canal and the Olympic Mountains. Comb the beach for oysters, fish from the dock, go for a row, or walk woodland lanes. A hearty breakfast is served (included), and lunch is offered to multinight guests, as is a prix-fixe dinner (open to nonguests on weekends by reservation). On Friday nights it's a salmon or chicken barbecue; on Saturdays, a lavish four-course dinner. The inn has a good selection of wines. It's about a half-hour drive here from the Bremerton ferry, although some guests opt to arrive by boat or floatplane. *2390 Tekiu Rd, Seabeck; 9 miles south of Seabeck; call or write for directions; 800/725-2600 or 360/830-4492; www.willcoxhouse.com; $$$; DIS, MC, V; checks OK.* ♿

## SILVERDALE

***When Captain Vancouver explored these parts in 1792, he missed Dyes Inlet, Liberty Bay, and Agate Pass altogether. So Silverdale had to wait until 1889 to be discovered—by real estate developers. The story goes that Silverdale's early city fathers wanted to name their town Goldendale, but the upstarts in Klickitat County had already claimed the name, so they settled for a slightly less precious metal.***

Silverdale, north of Bremerton on Dyes Inlet, is noted for the huge Kitsap Mall and all the shopping complexes it has spawned. But make your way through the commercial clutter down to Old Towne Silverdale, which has seen little need to change with the times. It is graced by a peaceful waterfront park at the end of Washington Street. The grassy haven has picnic tables, rest rooms, a rocky beach, a children's play area, a capacious picnic shelter, and a small wooden pavilion on a knoll from which to keep an eye on the kids at play. A long pier stretches out to floats with moorage for a dozen or so boats. It's hard to believe that Costco is only a mile away.

## ACTIVITIES

***Lunch Break.*** Stop at the Waterfront Park Bakery & Cafe (3472 Byron, across from the Old Town Pub; 360/698-2991), the self-dubbed "Center of the Known Universe for Coffee & Comfort" for lunch or take-out. Superior sandwiches, quiches, salads, and desserts are served in the tiny, spotless cafe, or at outdoor tables. You call the shots: if you so desire, add dilled chicken or Asian noodles to your basic green salad, or pesto to your veggie pizza.

***A Whale of a Festival.*** If you didn't get enough fireworks on the Fourth, head to Silverdale on the last weekend of July during the Whaling Days Festival, centered at Waterfront Park. (Never mind that Silverdale never had a whaling industry; any excuse for a party.) It all starts with a bang on Friday night with fireworks over the bay. Saturday the park is alive with music, fast-food booths, entertainers, and lots and lots of people out for a good time.

***Agate Pass, which separated the Kitsap Peninsula from Bainbridge Island until they built a bridge, was named not for the sought-after rock but for the artist on Charles Wilkes's 1841 exploring expedition, Alfred T. Agate.***

***A Park for All Ages.*** The J. A. & Anna Smith Children's Park, near Tracyton Boulevard and Fairgrounds Road, is a nice, family-friendly park with plenty to keep the kids happy, plus a bonus for grown-up gardeners: it houses the demonstration garden of local Master Gardeners. On Wednesdays they're on hand to give you a tour and answer questions.

## RESTAURANTS

### ALADDIN'S PALACE ★

Imagine, a genuine Lebanese restaurant flourishing in the commercial jungles of Silverdale. Begin your meal with such treats as falafel, tabbouleh, or *zahra* (deep-fried cauliflower with zesty tahini sauce). The house salad intrigues with its mint vinaigrette. Go on to shish kabob; plump well-stuffed dolmas; or a luscious moussaka studded with roasted garlic cloves. The dessert specialty is baklava, flaky and seductively sweet. Partner it with Arabian coffee, and you'll feel you've ascended to paradise. Some of Aladdin's items are available for take-out. *9399 Ridgetop Blvd NW, Suite B, Silverdale; corner of Ridgetop and Mickelberry; 360/698-6599; $$; AE, DC, DIS, MC, V; local checks only; lunch and dinner every day; full bar.*

### BAHN THAI ★★

Benchai (Benny) Sunti runs this restaurant, sister to the one in Seattle with the same name, with a similar menu, but a much different look. This is a place to come with a group of hungry eaters to share a wide variety of the brightly flavored dishes of Thailand. *Tod Mun*—spicy, crisp patties of minced fish, green beans, and lime leaves—is served with a contrasting fresh cucumber relish, making an excellent starter before *Tom Yum Goong,* a favorite Thai soup of prawns and lemon grass. Try one of six different exotic curries, including *Masuman*—beef and potatoes sauced with a mildly hot curry infused with coconut milk and cloves, nutmeg, and cinnamon. *9811 Mickleberry Rd, Silverdale; ½ block north of Bucklin Hill Rd; 360/698-3663; $; AE, MC, V; local checks only; lunch, dinner every day; full bar.* ♿

### HAKATA ★

For those searching for sushi with a difference, chef Yoshiyuki Sugimoto, formerly at Bush Gardens in Seattle, offers some intriguing selections in his own immaculate restaurant in an out-of-the-way shopping plaza. *Tobikko* (flying fish roe) and wasabi (pungent Japanese horseradish) explode with flavor when you bite through a handroll. A tangy leaf of shiso adds a subtle surprise to a delicate nigirisushi of flounder, and the spider roll—made with crunchy soft-shell crab—is a house favorite. In a class by itself is the fat, fancy futomaki roll with its pinwheel of contrasting ingredients. For lunch, try one of the popular meal-in-one dishes like donburi (big bowls of rice heaped with such delights as shrimp and vegetable tempura). *10876 Myhre Pl, #108, Silverdale; take the Kitsap Mall exit off Hwy 3, behind the post office in Pacific Linen Plaza; 360/698-0929; $; MC, V; local checks only; lunch Tues–Sat, dinner Tues–Sun; beer and wine.* ♿

### YACHT CLUB BROILER ★

View

This is a simple restaurant with some elegant touches and a water view, copper-covered tables, walls lined with delicate rice-paper fish prints, and bare wood floors softened by Oriental-style rugs. As might be expected by its name and location (on Dyes Inlet), seafood is a major menu item here. What is unexpected is the excellent quality of that seafood—sweet, moist Dungeness crab cakes, a bucket of plump steamed clams—as the commercial fishermen who eat here will attest. The prime rib special on Sunday and Monday nights makes scrumptious eating, too. *9226 Bayshore Dr, Silverdale; from Hwy 305 take the Silverdale exit, then the first right into town, then left on Bayshore; 360/698-*

*1601; $$; AE, DC, MC, V; checks OK; lunch, dinner every day, brunch Sun; full bar.* ♿

## LODGINGS

### WESTCOAST SILVERDALE HOTEL ☆

This resort hotel makes a good getaway destination despite its lures for conventioneers and conferences. Many rooms have balconies with views over Dyes Inlet; minisuites are the best. Extras include an indoor lap pool with sliding glass doors opening onto a large brick sundeck, a sauna, weight room, video-game room, tennis courts, and boat dock. The Mariner Grill offers white-linened tables, professional service, and nicely prepared meals that aren't too pricey. Salty Sam's Lounge is a favored hangout. Breakfast is par excellence, with boardinghouse-style biscuits and gravy or Belgian waffles piled with strawberries and cream. *3073 Bucklin Hill Rd, Silverdale; turn east at the intersection of Silverdale Way and Bucklin Hill Rd; 800/544-9799 or 360/698-1000; rrabourn@silverlink.net; www.westcoasthotels.com/silverdale; $$; AE, DIS, DC, MC, V; checks OK; breakfast, lunch, dinner every day; full bar.* ♿

***Tap your toes and bounce with the beat of the Navy Band Northwest concerts at the Naval Undersea Museum in Keyport, on fall and winter Sunday afternoons. Or come to the Saturday afternoon film series in the summer, same place, and get beneath the surface to see undersea volcanoes, submarine spy missions and more. It's all free; access num.kpt.nuwc.navy.mil, or call 360/396-4148.***

# KEYPORT

It looks like a sleepy little waterfront town, but its off-limits Naval Undersea Warfare Center makes it the second largest employer in Kitsap County, hence the nickname, "Torpedo Town USA."

## ACTIVITIES

***Under the Sea.*** Never mind the torpedoes, full speed ahead for the Naval Undersea Museum (PO Box 408, Keyport, WA; 360/697-1129). This imposing white block of a building on the right just as you enter Keyport is as shipshape as an admiral's flagship, and shows you more than you ever thought to ask about marine science, naval history, and evolving undersea technology. See dive suits seemingly designed for giants, a Japanese suicide torpedo, and the *Alvin,* a submersible whose feats include helping to recover an H-bomb lost in the Spanish seas, and which later helped investigate the *Titanic*. A new attraction is the *Sub-Human II*, a two-man-powered submarine that made the *Guinness Book of Records* for a speed record. One man pedals, the other steers. The museum is free, and open daily in summer, daily except Tuesdays in winter. The gift shop, a bit pricey, has largely tasteful and unusual wares. Pick up a cuddly stuffed puffin or a brass ship's barometer.

***Sandwich Stop.*** Pop in for a post-museum lunch or snack at Keyport Mercantile's sandwich shop (Washington and Grandview). Good food and a great view of the water.

## RESTAURANTS

### WHISKEY CREEK STEAKHOUSE

Come in and take a load off in this informal restaurant, evocative of a slightly gussied up Wild West saloon. Climb on a stool and yammer with Tom the bartender; gather with your pardners around a table well polished by many an elbow, innocent of cloth, candle, or flowers, and dig in. The dinner menu lists nine steak choices, from chicken-fried with country gravy to an 18-ounce porterhouse, as well as prime rib. And the steaks are very good indeed—hearty in size, tender and juicy, and just as rare or well done as you ordered. Non-steak eaters may choose among a dozen chicken and seafood offerings, some humble (fish and chips) and some ambitious (a creditable chicken cordon bleu with béarnaise sauce). Saddles and cowboy hats, a mounted steer head, and a back bar that came around the Cape get you in the mood. Step out on the deck, though, and you might be at a chic urban eatery. Owners Pat and Karan Ziarnik have added an open-air dining area bedecked with hanging baskets, vines, and greenery; one semienclosed section can be heated so outdoor dining is possible practically year-round. *1918 E Washington; PO Box 642, Keyport; on the left near the end of Washington St; 360/779-3481; $$; AE, MC, V; local checks only; lunch and dinner Mon–Sat, dinner Sun; full bar.*

## POULSBO

From the blue-balconied Sons of Norway Hall at one end of Front Street to the troll in front of the New Day Fishery at the other, this has to be "Little Norway on the Fjord." The route from the town center on Liberty Bay to Bainbridge Island is acquiring strip-mall accretions, but down by the water you're in a dolled-up village straight from the old country. Just think of today's pleasure boats moored in the harbor as the fishing boats of yesterday, and admire the colorful folk-art motifs sported by the shops. Even the North Kitsap Senior Center, gleaming with cream, blue, and silver, looks like a little Norwegian wedding cake. Up on the hill, the Faith Lutheran Church crowns the illusion with its tall blue-and-white steeple.

## ACTIVITIES

***Sweets and Treats.*** If there were still any doubt of the town's heritage, Sluys Bakery (18924 Front Street NE; 360/779-2798) would remove it, with its high-cholesterol Nordic pastries and dense, healthful Poulsbo Bread, famous far beyond the peninsula. The espresso is a good accompaniment if you succumb to a gooey goodie. A block away from Sluys Bakery more temptation lurks: Boehm's Chocolates, at the end of an innocent-looking passageway (18864 Front Street NE; 360/697-3318). Yield to an ice cream bar at least, or to a long-stemmed chocolate rose, $3.50 each.

***On the Waterfront.*** Like everything else in Poulsbo, the waterfront is tidy, compact, and visitor-friendly. Liberty Bay Park is generously furnished with picnic tables, rest rooms, and big rocks for kids to scramble over. Kvelstad Pavilion, with hewn timbers and carved wood trim, is a popular spot for weddings. A boardwalk runs along the shore, leading to the half-mile trail through the trees to American Legion Park, with picnic tables and a children's play area. Liberty Bay Park is the center for some of Poulsbo's most remarkable festivals—such as the early December Yule Fest when the Vikings come out to play. By torchlight, fur-clad figures with horned helmets, swords at the ready, march to the dock to welcome Lucia Bride, who arrives by boat.

Everyone gathers at Kvelstad Pavilion to light the Yule Log, cheer and yell, and the Norwegian holiday season is properly launched.

***Make Friends with a Sea Cucumber.*** The Marine Science Center (215 Third Avenue S; 360/779-5549) offers hands-on encounters with friendly sea creatures like starfish, anemones, and sand dollars. If you or your children have never hand-fed a crab, now's your chance. Open daily.

***Gazebo Cafe.*** Watch the world go by and have a bowl of soup while perched on a stool at the open-air counter in front of the cafe (18830 Front Street NE; 360/697-1447). Or eat on the patio, or order take-out. The bread's made in-house and the veggies are fresh; the bratwurst and Wiener schnitzel taste wonderfully authentic.

***Olympic Outdoor Center.*** This is the local outfitter for bluewater and whitewater adventures. Rent a canoe or kayak for an hour or so and paddle around Liberty Bay, watching the seals haul out on the breakwater (don't get too close and alarm them). 18971 Front Street NE; 360/697-6095.

## RESTAURANTS

### JJ'S FISH HOUSE ★

Like a Mediterranean bistro that sprawls out onto the sidewalk on fine days, JJ's (for Jeff and Judy Eagleson) seizes the moment when the sun shines and opens up the big doors. The inside space is wide open too, with views of Poulsbo's animated waterfront and Liberty Bay beyond. Opt for an intimate booth, or perch at the counter and watch the chefs, stirring and sautéeing away. The seafood menu is as far-ranging as the milieu. The clam chowder might not please purists (heavy on potato and bacon) but the cioppino, made to order for each serving, is loaded with shellfish and chunks of halibut, and the herbed broth is heavenly. The warmed sourdough bread comes in a lidded basket, the cheerful young waitstaff in their nautical bluejeans and white T-shirts are attentive, and all is as it should be in this mellow waterfront restaurant. *18881 Front St, PO Box 2628, Poulsbo; north side of the main waterfront street; 360/779-*

*6609; $$; AE, MC, V; checks OK; lunch and dinner every day; beer and wine.*

### MOLLY WARD GARDENS ★★

Sam and Lynn Ward's homespun establishment shines best when the sun does—when the open French doors welcome the garden scents, when the chefs can forage in the organic garden, and when you and your friends have time to savor the experience, maybe even wander through the garden between courses. Lunch on the sunny patio could easily take up a whole afternoon. Whatever is served (it's decided at Sam's whim) will be accompanied by delicate garden-vegetable soup and freshly picked greens. *27462 Big Valley Road, Poulsbo; just north of Manor Farm Inn on the east side of Big Valley Rd; 360/779-4471; $$; MC, V; checks OK; lunch Tues–Sat, dinner Wed–Mon, brunch Sun; beer and wine.*

## LODGINGS

### MANOR FARM INN ★★

A lavish retreat in the middle of nowhere, Manor Farm is a real farm with horses, sheep, chickens, and a trout pond—a beguiling mix of country and sophistication that succeeds in spoiling even the city-bred. New owners Suzanne and Christopher Plemmons and Christopher's mother Janet Plemmons maintain the high standards of longtime innkeeper Jill Hughes. Breakfast still happens twice at Manor Farm: first a tray of hot scones and orange juice is left at your door, then from 8:30 to 10:30 the real farm breakfast is served in the dining room: perhaps Eggs Benedict Dungeness (served atop Dungeness crab) or a Puget Platter Scramble—eggs scrambled with lox, red onion, and Swiss cheese. The new innkeepers have added a restaurant, Christopher's at the Inn, open to the public as well as guests, serving breakfast and dinner seven days a week. The impressive dinner menu lists half a dozen entrees, including smoking duck salad, with a hot bacon–brown sugar dressing; and flank steak chimichurri. Sunday night suppers are prix fixe, with a simpler menu. We believe Christopher's at the Inn will find a niche in the Kitsap Peninsula scene, and will be watching it closely. The seven bright guest rooms are beautifully comfortable; two have fireplaces. The inn offers croquet and horseshoes on the spacious grounds, and lends bikes to guests. *26069 Big Valley Rd NE, Poulsbo; ½ hour from Winslow ferry dock off Hwy 3 on Big Valley Rd; 360/779-4628; $$$; AE, MC, V; checks OK; breakfast every day, dinner Wed–Sat, supper Sun; beer and wine.*

## SUQUAMISH

A pair of evocative Indian heritage sites are near Suquamish, just down the road from Poulsbo, on the west side of Agate Pass. Old Man House State Park commemorates the site of a long-gone Suquamish longhouse, burnt by the U.S. government in an effort to civilize the Indians. It's believed to have been the largest such structure ever built: 900 feet long and 60 feet wide. The park has a sandy beach, picnic tables, and an informational display telling about this moving chapter in Native American history. The grave of Chief Sealth, for whom Seattle was named, is in a cemetery between the park and the town of Suquamish. A sign on the path quotes his exhortation to "love this beautiful land."

## ACTIVITIES

***Suquamish Museum.*** This handsome free museum, off Highway 305 just west of the Agate Pass Bridge near the Suquamish Clearwater Casino, evokes a vanished way of life with dramatic exhibits and a poignant video of tribal elders' memories, *Come Forth Laughing: Voices of the Suquamish People.* The gift shop offers books on Native American life and history, and authentic arts and crafts. Picnic tables outside overlook the water and a pleasant nature trail winds through the trees. The museum welcomes school tours and groups who wish to schedule salmon feasts, receptions, and such. Open daily in summer, weekends in winter. 15838 Sandy Hook Rd, PO Box 498, Suquamish; 360/598-3311.

## KINGSTON

Most visitors to the peninsula see Kingston only fleetingly. Arriving via the Edmonds ferry, they drive quickly through it on their way to somewhere else. Departing, they see it as a parking lot where you wait for the ferry, and woe betide you if you stray too far from your car. Now there's an incentive to stay on the dock: a handsome new overlook on the bluff from which to watch for your ferry, admire the view, and take a short stroll down to the beach.

***Take a side trip to a Mosquito Fleet port. Drive south from Kingston to Indianola, a reclusive community that would just as soon be left alone. Until 1950, it had its own dock for ferries to Seattle. Now the 300-yard pier has been rebuilt. You're welcome to walk out to fish or to admire the cross-sound view, but the beach is private.***

## ACTIVITIES

***Boaters' Safe Haven.*** Mariners, who can be more leisurely than motorists, have long appreciated Kingston for its marina—the only sheltered moorage on Kitsap Peninsula's northeast stretch. North of here, beaches are wild and unwelcoming. Appletree Cove, just west of the ferry terminal, has full facilities and room for 40 boats. There's even a little park with picnic tables.

***Joe on the Go.*** Just half a block up from the ferry, a modest espresso place, Coffee Exchange (11229 NE State Highway 104; 360/297-7817) is handy for ferry travelers. Good pastries, too, and a few tables for lingerers. They roast their own coffee and sell beans.

## RESTAURANTS

### KINGSTON HOTEL CAFE ☆☆

At this snug eatery near the ferry Judith Weinstock serves a cuisine that abounds in freshness, ethnic influences, and imagination and has enslaved ferry travelers and locals who crowd the little cafe from morning to night. Have your latte with a strawberry scone, heavenly and light, on the porch with its view of the Seattle skyline across the Sound, or in winter cozy up to the wood stove with a bowl of roasted apple-ginger bisque. Seafood is a good choice year-round, such as halibut cakes topped with mango chutney or a fish stew rich with mussels, clam, and halibut—a dinner appetizer that could serve as a light meal. Baked goods are always warm and fresh. A charming garden patio in back sometimes takes the cafe overflow or catered events, and gives the kids a place to play while you linger over your meal. Step upstairs to visit David Weinstock in his custom jewelry studio if you like. *25931 Washington Blvd; at 1st Ave, 1 block north of ferry terminal; 360/297-8100; $; MC, V; checks OK; brunch Fri–Sun, dinner every day; beer and wine.*

## HANSVILLE

As fishing has declined, the doughty old resorts at this tiny end-of-the-road community near Point No Point, northwest of Kingston, have disappeared or lapsed into decrepitude. Present-day Hansville centers on the Hansville Grocery & Provisions Co., 7532 NE Twin Spits Road; 360/638-2303, fax 360/638-1400. Here you may stock up on food, books, local gossip, beer, wine, and videos—and send a fax or make a copy. The town has no restaurant, but this is picnic country.

## ACTIVITIES

***That huge rock on the beach, near the stairs up to the county park, is an erratic—a boulder dropped by an ancient glacier as it ground its way over Puget Sound during the last Ice Age.***

***On the Beach.*** The stubby Coast Guard lighthouse at the end of the sandy spit still flashes, and still welcomes visitors (call for tour information; 360/638-2261). Walk the miles of beach south of the lighthouse, but don't trespass on residents' property; only the beach below mean high water level is public. Still, at low tide there's plenty of play area for the kids, and driftwood logs to lean against for a snooze or inspection of maritime activity in Admiralty Inlet. Along the way, a rustic stairway climbs through the woods to Point No Point County Park.

***Lakeside Park.*** A five-minute drive up the hill behind Hansville leads to Buck Lake County Park, a delightful surprise hidden in the woods. The grassy slope is dotted with picnic tables and barbecue grills. You'll find a picnic shelter, slides and swings, rest rooms, even showers. In summer the lake is swimmable. Fishermen angle here for trout and bass.

***Foulweather Bluff Nature Preserve.*** It takes some doing to find this Nature Conservancy preserve. Head about 3 miles west of Hansville on Twin Spits Road, 0.2 mile before the Skunk Bay Road intersection, watch for an inconspicuous sign on a tree on the left side of the road. If the sign isn't there, take the trail that's flanked by two big alders, and when you come to a big sign with the rules of the preserve, you know you're on the right track. The trail wanders through groves of alder and cedar and leads to a marsh, separated from Hood Canal by a natural sand berm. This 93-acre preserve, a rare combination of forest, marsh, beach, and sea, has something for every nature enthusiast. Listen for pileated woodpeckers in the woods and watch great blue herons stalk their prey in the bulrushes. Along the 3,700-foot-long beach, look for grebes, bufflehead, and other seabirds in the bay. At low tide, peer into the tidepools. But be respectful: no clam digging, pets, smoking, fires, vehicles, bikes, or horses. The preserve closes at dusk.

## LODGINGS

### GUEST HOUSE ★

View It's a real find at this far corner of the Kitsap Peninsula, west of Hansville near Foulweather Bluff (Captain Vancouver didn't like the rainstorm he ran into here, hence the name). The Guest House is just the place to snuggle down and watch winter storms, or have a lazy summertime retreat. The house is the sole survivor of long-gone Twin Spits Resort, but a far cry from those rugged days. It's been completely rebuilt and fitted out by Norma and Leon Thomas, and has a tremendous view of the Olympic Mountains across the water, with a deck to make the most of it and absolute privacy and peace. You haven't seen an Olympic sunset until you've seen it from here. The house includes a living room, full kitchen, fireplace, TV, and a bedroom with queen plus hideabed; if your party overflows the space, you may rent an adjoining twin-bedded guest bedroom with its own entrance. It's a comfortable walk from the Guest House, by road or beach, to the nature preserve. *2570 NE Twin Spits Rd, Hansville; 2 miles from Hansville on Twin Spits Rd; 360/638-1001; ghtwinspit@aol.com; $$; no credit cards; checks OK.*

## PORT GAMBLE

Since the Pope and Talbot mill—long touted as North America's oldest continually operating lumber mill—closed, rumors are

*Of Sea and Shore Museum, sprawling around the balcony in the Port Gamble General Store, displays more than 14,000 shells and marine fossils from all over the world.*

rife about the future of the company town. For now, it remains as it was. Drive along its maple-shaded streets lined with immaculate, perfectly preserved 19th century homes and you will feel like you're in a New England village. In fact, the whole town was modeled after the Pope and Talbot founders' home of East Mochias, Maine, and is now a National Historic Site. There's hardly a more inviting picnic spot in the county than its grassy expanses with their panoramic views of the old mill and the water.

## ACTIVITIES

***Port Gamble Historic Museum.*** In this gem of a museum, half a block north of Highway 104 in the center of town, relive Port Gamble's timber-nurtured past. See re-creations of a ship's cabin, a sawdusty mill room, the lushly decorated lobby of the late Hotel Puget, and an Indian longhouse. Sound effects add to the illusions: waves lapping at the porthole, the buzzing of circular saws. Open daily, 10am to 4pm, Memorial Day through Labor Day; closed in winter except by appointment; 360/297-8074.

***Real Live Company Store.*** The Port Gamble General Store (1 Rainier Avenue; 360/297-2623) still opens its creaky doors as it has done for a century and more. Located above the historical museum, it's the only store in town—just the place if you've been looking for a galvanized washtub or a kerosene lantern, or for more mundane items such as groceries. You'll find espresso, soups, deli sandwiches, and mile-high ice cream cones.

***Kitsap Memorial State Park.*** This popular stop, off Highway 3 and three miles south of the east end of the Hood Canal Bridge, is an ideal spot to take a break during a journey. You can turn the kids loose on swings and playfields, have a picnic, wander the beach, or just stretch your legs. There are 43 campsites, as well as picnic shelters for groups. Many a family reunion takes place here. Reserve by calling 360/779-3205.

# OLYMPIC PENINSULA

# NORTHEAST CORNER

Beyond Hood Canal the true Olympic Peninsula begins. The northeast corner, a minipeninsula in itself, wears its history on its sleeve. Travelers are invited to visit a lavish resort based on a timber tycoon's domain (Port Ludlow), and one of the best-preserved Victorian towns on the West Coast (Port Townsend), where arts, entertainment, and cuisine are taken as seriously as the gingerbread-lavished architecture. Opportunities abound for outdoor activities, from kayaking to hiking, bird-watching to beachcombing. Besides all its on-the-spot attractions, this corner of the Olympic Peninsula is only about 50 miles from a major gateway to Olympic National Park. What a delightful idea: have dinner at a luxe restaurant with a view, spend the night in pampered comfort at a cozy inn, and after a waistband-stretching breakfast, go west. By midafternoon you could be hiking a trail at Hurricane Ridge or rafting the Elwha.

## ACTIVITIES

***Bird-Watching Beach.*** At the west end of Hood Canal Bridge on Bywater Bay is one of the Olympic Peninsula's least-known and least-developed parks, good for beach walking and superb for bird-watching. Take the first right after you leave the bridge onto Ludlow-Paradise Road; take a right on Seven Sisters Road; drive half a mile to a small parking area where there is access to Wolfe Property Park. An easy hike along the beach leads to where, at low or preferably minus tide, you can wade across the lagoon to North Spit. Walk along the spit to Hood Head—the whale-shaped island you saw from the bridge.

***Chamber Music in the Barn.*** You haven't heard Mozart until you've taken in a performance at the Olympic Music Festival's summer concerts in a barn-turned-concert hall. On Highway 104, drive 10 miles west from the Hood Canal Bridge, take the Chimacum-Center Road exit, and drive half a mile south. Members of the Philadelphia String Quartet, joined by noted artists from around the world, play in the turn-of-the-century dairy barn; listeners sit inside on hay bales or padded church pews or (for a little less) on the lawn outside, in which case a blanket or lawn chair is a good idea. You're encouraged to come early

***Port Ludlow's 27-hole golf course attracts golfers who want a challenge and don't mind a view; it's been called the country's most scenic by the Society of Golf Course Architects.***

and wander the 55-acre farm, let the kids meet the donkeys, and have a picnic. Bring your own or buy something at the Milking Shed: sandwiches, ice cream, desserts, and beverages (including local wines and beers). Or call ahead and reserve a box lunch. Concerts are at 2pm, Saturdays and Sundays, from June through Labor Day; 206/527-8839.

## PORT LUDLOW

Here on Paradise Bay off Admiralty Inlet, there's virtually nothing left of the ostentatious Pope and Talbot kingdom that grew around the flourishing timber and lumber operations in the late 1800s. Now a 3,000-acre resort complex attracts pleasure lovers, who come to stay in the luxurious lodgings, dine, golf, and maybe buy a condominium or build a house.

## LODGINGS

### HERON BEACH INN ★★

View Heron Beach Inn (formerly The Inn at Ludlow Bay and a sister establishment to Pam and Paul Schell's Inn at Langley and Friday Harbor House) guards the head of Hood Canal on a sandy bar across from the Resort at Port Ludlow. It exudes the atmosphere of a New England estate; inside is a gorgeous, peaceful retreat with 37 big, well-appointed rooms with fireplaces, great views, and deep tubs. You can play chess in the living room, or hold your own private wine-tasting in front of a blazing fire. The inn's restaurant has a pleasing ambience that makes good food taste even better. *One Heron Rd, PO Box 65460, Port Ludlow; 6 miles north of west end of Hood Canal Bridge via Ludlow-Paradise Rd; 360/437-0411; $$$; AE, DIS, MC, V; checks OK; lunch Wed–Sun, dinner every day.* ♿

### PORT LUDLOW RESORT AND CONFERENCE CENTER ★

View Pope and Talbot's 1880s sawmill manager situated his long-gone "biggest damn cabin on the Sound" on this magnificent site overlooking the bay. Still owned by Pope and Talbot, it is now a popular resort facility catering especially to groups, with a marina, tennis courts, 27-hole championship golf course, hiking and cycling trails, and year-round swimming pool, all on 1,500 developed acres. The individually decorated suites—all privately owned as second homes by out-of-town families—offer fireplaces, kitchens, and private decks, many with views of the harbor. Stay away from the standard rooms, which resemble those of a budget motel. The Harbormaster Restaurant (open daily for breakfast, lunch, and dinner) has a pleasant bar and a delightful deck. *200 Olympic Pl, Port Ludlow; 6 miles north of west end of Hood Canal Bridge via Ludlow-Paradise Rd; 800/732-1239 or 360/437-2222; www.portludlowresort.com; $$$; AE, MC, V; checks OK.*

***Along Highway 19 between Port Ludlow and Port Townsend you pass through little Chimacum, home of the locally beloved Chimacum Cafe (4900 Rhody Drive; 360/732-4631). You'll enjoy the folksy hospitality and wonderful basics like meat loaf, fish and chips, steaks, and oysters.***

## PORT HADLOCK

This onetime mill town, about halfway between Port Ludlow and Port Townsend, comprises Upper Hadlock and Lower Hadlock. The former is noted for its locksmith (Hadlock Padlock), the latter for the Ajax Cafe (described below), for its commanding position at the approach to Indian and Marrowstone Islands, and for what is probably the country's only resort created out of a deserted alcohol plant.

## ACTIVITIES

***Fresh and Organic.*** Swan Farms (Highway 19 and Nesses Corner Road, Port Hadlock; 360/385-6365) is much more than just another roadside grocery. Farm-fresh, locally grown produce is heaped in bins outside; inside, the most serious searcher for organic, natural foods will have a field day. So will anyone ready for lunch: a tiny cafe in the back serves up bowls of flavorful homemade soups, sandwiches to order, and yummy pies and muffins. Wander through the herb garden to see where some of those flavors came from. Walk a few steps along and there's the Village Baker, creator of some of the Olympic Peninsula's most highly regarded bread. If you're lucky, it'll be the day for walnut-olive.

## RESTAURANTS

### AJAX CAFE

The old-timers living in Port Townsend, Port Ludlow, and points in between have cheered every time this longtime eating establishment, despite acquiring new owners, didn't change much. The cafe still has a style all its own: waterfront-funky. The Mediterranean seafood stew, served in copious portions with garlic aioli, is famous. So are the Black Jack barbecued pork ribs (Jack Daniel's, that is). Live music, weekends. *271 Water St, Port Hadlock; in Lower Hadlock on the waterfront, off Oak Bay Rd; 360/385-3450; $$; MC, V; local checks only; dinner Tues–Sun; beer and wine.*

## LODGINGS

### THE OLD ALCOHOL PLANT

Its career as a producer of industrial alcohol was brief (1910–1913), but after 65 years of abandonment it was thoroughly rebuilt and took on new life as a hotel and marina. It looks vaguely Spanish, with a red-tiled roof and, inside, high beamed ceilings and brick walls. All 25 rooms have private baths; a few suites have kitchens. The restaurant serves breakfast, lunch, and dinner on weekends; dinner only, Thursday-Sunday (subject to change—call ahead). Prices for most rooms are modest but the view is not—an expansive vista of marina, bay, and islands, with Port Townsend to the north. Splurgers may go all out and stay in the two-story penthouse suite—a spacious apartment with elevator access, kitchen, dining room, and living room—that sleeps five. *310 Alcohol Loop Dr, Port Hadlock; about one mile from Port Hadlock via Oak Bay Rd; 800/785-7030 or 360/385-7030; $-$$$; AE, DC, DIS, MC, V; checks OK; full bar; www.alcoholplant@olympus.net.*

# MARROWSTONE ISLAND

Reach this rural eastern bit of Jefferson County by driving to Port Hadlock, then across the bridge and the southern end of Indian Island (a naval reservation, securely fenced). Fort Flagler, at Marrowstone's north end, was a companion to Fort Worden and Fort Casey at the end of the last century, bristling with armaments. It's on the National Register of Historic Places and within sight of Fort Flagler State Park, a favorite of nature lovers. It commands sensational three-way water views and offers camping, picnicking, miles of hiking trails, and a nature preserve. A large group of seals are on home turf at the end of the sandspit.

## ACTIVITIES

***Fort Flagler Hostel.*** Groups like Olympic Park Institute and North Cascades Institute sometimes hold seminars at the Fort Flagler Hostel, and individuals are welcome too. Lodgings are dorm-style in bunks, and there's a room just for families. The big living room has a woodstove and there are group cooking facilities. Lodgings are as cheap as the views outside are rich. Come by bike and pay less. It's open March through September, at 10621 Flagler Road, Nordland; 360/385-3701.

## LODGINGS

### THE ECOLOGIC PLACE

A great spot for families who'd rather spend more time out than in, this is your basic gathering of rustic cabins in a natural setting. And what a setting! The Ecologic Place has 2 miles of beachfront, bordering on a tidal estuary that flows into Oak Bay and then Puget Sound, and offers a view of the Olympics and Mount Rainier, conditions permitting. The eight cabins, each with its own character, have never known an interior decorator, but have everything you need to enjoy the simple beauty of the place—woodstoves, equipped kitchens, comfortable queen-size beds, and fine-for-the-children bunks and twins. Bring bikes, books, bathing suits, binoculars, and grub. Launch a boat, go kayaking, look for an osprey. *10 Beach Dr, Nordland; turn right at "Welcome to Marrowstone" sign; 800/871-3077 or 360/385-3077; www.ecologicplace.com; $$; MC, V; checks OK.*

***Just ask, and someone will tell you how to find Egg and I Road, where Betty MacDonald lived and wrote her biting memoir of Port Townsend.***

# PORT TOWNSEND

Port Townsend is an ever-changing mix of quaint and quirky, with an enduring backdrop of ornate 1890s-era architecture. A stroll along Water Street, the main downtown route, offers shoppers a mixed bag, from souvenir mugs to antique ship models to environmentally correct clothing and food. There's a connoisseur's assortment of galleries, fine shops, bookstores, and highly regarded restaurants. Marinas attract day sailors, yachts, and fishing boats, while the chunky little ferries faithfully ply their way to and from Whidbey Island. Along the waterfront, restaurants and small parks command beautiful views, from Mount Baker to Mount Rainier. Above all this, handsome mansions on the bluff—many converted to bed-and-breakfasts—mark the domain of the 19th-century merchants and tycoons who built as far away from the hurly-burly of the waterfront as they could. A few blocks away on Lawrence Street, pizzerias and espresso bars proliferate. To get a handle on all this, pick up a comprehensive guide to historic homes and buildings at the Visitor Information Center as you drive into town (2437 Sims Way; 360/385-2722). But consider leaving your car on the outskirts: Port Townsend is very walkable but not always parkable. A free shuttle leaves every half-hour from the Park & Ride (Haines Street and Sims Way, near Safeway) to run uptown along Lawrence, then down to Water Street and back to the Park & Ride. You may get off at any time, poke about, and board a later bus.

## ACTIVITIES

***Jefferson County Historical Society Museum.*** A three-story compendium of artifacts, photos, displays, and oddments, Jefferson County Historical Society Museum (210 Madison Street; 360/385-1003) offers varied exhibits, from mementos of the early Chinese settlers to an authentic Victorian bedroom. Below it all, a gloomy dungeon room is said to be where Jack London spent a night on his way to the Klondike. Donation; open daily.

***Chetzemoka Park.*** Named for Chief Chetzemoka, "the friend of the pioneer," this is the oldest park in town: a 10-acre grassy tract where a few enormous firs remind us that this was once virgin forest. The picnic tables come with a view of Admiralty Inlet, the swings and slides keep the tots entertained, there's a charming rose arbor, and in summer bands hold forth in the gazebo. Paths lead down over the bluff to the beach and clamming. It's just a few minutes from downtown Port Townsend at 900 Jackson Street.

***Port Townsend, Washington; Galveston, Texas; and Cape May, New Jersey, are the only three Victorian seaports on the National Register listed as National Historic Landmarks.***

***Rothschild House Park.*** Built by a prominent merchant and now billed as Washington's smallest state park, this fine 1868 home is open for tours daily in summer, weekends in winter. Halfway up the hill on Jefferson at Taylor, it commands a sweeping view of downtown Port Townsend and the harbor. Stroll and sniff your way through the restored herb garden and flower garden. Donation; 360/385-4730.

***Fort Worden State Park.*** Two miles north of town, Fort Worden was built in the early 1900s as part of Puget Sound's harbor defense system. Now its 434 acres encompass a theater, hostels for students and elders, former officers' homes for rent (see review below), woodsy trails and beach walks, and the great green Parade Ground where nobody is told to keep off the grass. Clamber over Artillery Hill with its batteries and bunkers, peacefully retired after guarding Puget Sound from 1907 to 1953—without firing a shot. Take a guided tour through the elegant Commanding Officer's House (donation). The beach has 80 campsites, from full-utility to primitive; call 360/385-4730 to reserve. A step up the scale in lodging is the Olympic Hostel near the Parade Ground: private rooms with bedding (not linens) provided and a community kitchen and common room; 360/385-0655 or e-mail olyhost@olympus.net.

***On the way into town, just past the Safeway and opposite the marina, is one of the ten most important wildlife habitats in the state: Kah Tai Lagoon Park, rich in native plants and favored by bird-watchers. Venture in to find paths through meadows, picnic tables, a fitness trail, and rest rooms.***

***Show and Tell Sea Life.*** Down on the beach, at the Marine Science Center at the end of a long pier, touch tanks and aquaria gurgle away, filled with fascinating sea animals and plants. It's a hands-on place to learn all about eelgrass, what a sea star's feet feel like, and how an octopus has dinner. Nearby shores are prime bird-watching spots; summer brings rhinoceros auklets, pigeon guillemots, and the occasional tufted puffin. Sign up at the center for guided beach walks and marine interpretive programs. Bring the family to the Low Tide Fest in July—fish printing, scuba and kayak demonstrations, storytelling, and

***The spring and fall Historic Homes Tours, 360/385-2722, when a half-dozen historic homes are opened in all their 1890s glory, let you peek into the past. Several of Port Townsend's bed and breakfasts are usually included—a good chance to inspect the premises before you reserve your spot.***

plenty of other activities for the kids. Call 360/385-5582 or e-mail ptmsc@olympus.net.

***Seagoing Adventures.*** Go bird-watching and whale watching on the high seas on the *Glacier Spirit* with Puget Sound Express (431 Water Street; 360/385-5288; psexpres@olympus.net). The vessel sails daily, April 1 to mid-October, from Point Hudson to Friday Harbor and back, with a four-hour stopover. Second-generation Captain Pete's narration covers island history, scenery, and wildlife. Munch and sip as you go; the galley offers snacks, fresh-baked cinnamon rolls, soft drinks, coffee, beer, and wine.

***Centrum.*** For 27 years this nonprofit center for the arts and education has been dazzling its ever-growing public with entertainment and cultural enrichment. Headquartered at Fort Worden State Park, Centrum offers a profusion of performances, seminars, workshops, and concerts in idyllic settings. Among the summer offerings: the Seattle Symphony, Country Blues Festival, Festival of American Fiddle Tunes, Jazz Port Townsend, and Marrowstone Music Festival. The Port Townsend Writers' Conference is a July fixture. Performance venues include the McCurdy Pavilion, a dramatic remodeled structure that housed observation balloons in the 1920s; the adjacent Littlefield Green, where you may relax and listen in the sun; the more intimate Joseph F. Wheeler Theatre; and, during the blues and jazz festivals, clubs and pubs all over Port Townsend host performances. For schedules and information: Centrum, PO Box 1158, Port Townsend; 800/733-3608 or 360/385-3102; www.centrum.

***Blossoms and Boats.*** Port Townsend is always ready for a celebration. One of the most durable is the Rhododendron Festival; 360/385-2722. It bursts out in May, when the woods are splashed with showy pink blooms and the locals feel it's their turn to have some fun before summer's crowds invade. For a week, the town overflows with silly races and parades (trikes, dogs, and beds), arts and crafts fairs, the Rhody Run, and the grand parade with floats, royalty, marching bands, and freelance exhibitionists. Book your lodgings early—it has quite a following among festival connoisseurs. The Wooden Boat Festival (Wooden Boat Foundation; 360/385-3628), held the first weekend after Labor Day, is a jolly event, even if you're not a boater. It's centered at Point Hudson, at the end of Water Street, but things go on all over town and include jazz concerts, crafts shows, and strolling entertainers. Test-drive a dinghy or watch a sailboat regatta in the bay. If she's in port, tour the *Lady Washington*, a replica of Captain Robert Gray's 1878 flagship.

***Sweet-tooth ache? Pick up the town's best pastries at Bread and Roses Bakery (230 Water Street; 360/385-1044).***

SHOPS ***Strolling the Shops.*** Imprint Bookstore (820 Water Street; 360/385-3643) is well stocked with the latest guidebooks and nature books for your peninsula explorations. Upstairs from the bookstore, the Bruskin Gallery is a quiet space where you might be the first to discover an about-to-be-discovered Northwest artist. William James Bookseller (829 Water Street; 360/385-7313) has a vast selection of used books. For antiques, it's the Antique Mall (802 Water Street; 360/385-2590), where some 40 purveyors of old things have convened under one roof, offering fishing lures, toys, coins, jewelry, first editions, and you name it. Below it all, there's a display of Chinese artifacts excavated from the buried homes of the Chinese colony that flourished here in the 1890s. Earthenworks (702 Water Street; 360/385-0328) specializes in high-quality Washington craft items.

***Cool Treats.*** The Elevated Ice Cream Company has homemade ice cream cones and sundaes in dozens of flavors and colors, plus espresso, all offered in a roomy, well-scrubbed space where kids can be let loose. At the back, a sun deck is elevated just enough to give fine views of people on the pier and activity in the bay (627 Water Street; 360/385-1156). At Nifty Fiftys (817 Water Street; 360/385-1931) nostalgia rules, with a marble soda fountain, 1952 jukebox, gum machine, fountain drinks like egg creams and root beer floats, and ice cream concoctions like tin-roof sundaes and banana splits.

***The Wines of Water Street.*** At the Wine Seller (940 Water Street; 360/385-7673), browse the bins, pick up a bottle or a case from the huge selection, or buy gourmet snacks for a picnic. Also available: exotic beers, teas, and Pegasus coffee (roasted on Bainbridge Island).

***Laid-Back Lunch.*** Old sea dogs, young salts, and folks with time to kill hang out at the Landfall (412 Water Street;

360/385-5814). There's no better spot for sidelines supervision of the activity at the Point Hudson Marina across the road. The faded white restaurant has a slightly disreputable air—you wouldn't be surprised to see Long John Silver come stomping in. Three meals a day (except in winter, when it's only breakfast and lunch) are served at long, bare tables with benches; plenty of room to spread out your newspaper. Fare is standard but tasty: burgers, sandwiches, and salads, plus some Mexican choices, with beer and wine.

***Hidden Pub.*** Siren's (823 Water Street; 360/379-1100), hidden way up three flights of stairs in the historic Bartlett Building, is a delightful place to enjoy a glass of wine, have a snack, and listen to music from the bay view deck.

***While you're uptown, stroll over to the Jefferson County Courthouse, the big brick building at Jefferson and Walker with the 100-foot clock tower that dominates the skyline and gives mariners a homing landmark. It's one of the two oldest courthouses in the state. And you can set your watch by the clock.***

***Hoof It.*** One way to reach uptown is to climb the steep stairway at Taylor and Washington Streets, heralded by the voluptuous Haller Fountain. A gift to the city in 1906, the fountain features a naked lady, known variously as Galatea, Venus, or Innocence. While pranksters occasionally transform her into a Maidenform model. From the top of the stairs, it's another couple of blocks and you're on the bluff. This is bed-and-breakfast-land, where every other block seems to flaunt a handsomely restored home, embellished with gingerbread, turrets, and gables. Here, too, is St. Paul's, the oldest and possibly most picture-perfect church in the Episcopal Diocese of Olympia (after tiny St. Peter's in Tacoma). The white, steepled little structure perches on the bluff at Jefferson and Tyler Streets. Nearby, the Old Bell Tower (1906), whose bell used to summon firemen from near and far, lives out its days peacefully in a minipark.

***Upscale Uptown Grocery.*** Aldrich's Market (Lawrence and Tyler Streets; 360/385-0500) is an authentic 1890s general store with an upscale twist: very fresh seafood, organically grown produce, and a deli with seven kinds of sausages and excellent soups. Locally roasted coffees rub elbows with hand-dipped candles, smoked salmon, and good wines for under $10. Stock up here for your picnic at Chetzemoka Park.

***Kayak Port Townsend.*** With this experienced kayak outfitter, you can rent a kayak, explore nearby waters and isles on a half- or full-day guided paddle, or pick an overnight with hikes thrown in. You can also custom-design your own tour, maybe to Baja to look for whales. No children under 10. The current senior paddler is 84; anyone older can come free. 435 Water Street; PO Box 1387, Port Townsend; 360/385-6240.

***Every August, the Lawrence Street neighborhood becomes "Uptownsend," when the Uptown Community Street Fair takes place. Besides shaking a leg in a contra dance, one may judge the sidewalk chalk art, inspect arts and crafts, and watch the parade.***

***Best Megamountain View.*** Pick a table on the old ferry dock, grab your fish and chips and chowder at the Silverwater Fish and Chips Shack at the end of Quincy Street, and get set for a season in the sun—or at least for an afternoon. Mount Baker, the Cascades, and Mount Rainier beam at you as the waves lap at the pilings. Kids can cavort nearby at the Jackson Bequest Park.

***Northwest Native Art.*** High-quality Native American art is on view and for sale at three downtown galleries. Northwest Native Expressions (637 Water Street; 360/385-4770) is a Jamestown S'Klallam tribal enterprise, in a small two-level setting next to the lobby of the Waterstreet Hotel. It features baskets, drums, prints, jewelry, Salish blankets, plus books and notepaper. Nearly half the art, both traditional and contemporary, is from the Olympic Peninsula. North by Northwest (918 Water Street, Port Townsend; 360/385-0955) shows mostly Northwest or Eskimo art such as cedar and ivory carvings, bentwood boxes, and masks, and also displays Southwest objects like Navajo rugs, Casa Grande pottery, and Kachina dolls. Ancestral Spirits Gallery (701 Water Street; 360/385-0078) features Inuit carvings of bone, stone, and horn, and art from the northern coast.

***Over the Waves by Taxi.*** See Port Townsend from sea level with Water Taxi (Boat Haven Fuel Dock or Point Hudson Long Dock; 360/379-3258). Take a leisurely one-hour tour of the waterfront on Wednesday through Sunday afternoons ($6; $5 for seniors; $3 for 12 and under) or a three-hour morning tour, Wednesday through Saturday, to Indian and Marrowstone Islands with a stop at Nordland General Store ($18). The taxi, a onetime motor launch on the USS *Saratoga,* operates from mid-May to mid-September.

***Point Hudson Motel, Marina, and RV Park.*** A derelict Coast Guard station at the east tip of town was transformed into a resort in 1970, and it keeps evolving. The 24-room

*Between Point Hudson Motel and the beach is a genuine Makah canoe, marking the approximate spot where Captain George Vancouver came ashore in 1792.*

oft-remodeled motel is nothing fancy but there's plenty to do outside: watch the goings-on in the marina, walk the beach, or head for downtown Port Townsend, a few blocks away. The sprawl of peak-roofed, clapboard buildings includes a sailmaker, laundry, meeting pavilion, the Shanghai Restaurant (360/385-4810), and Otter Crossing, a little breakfast, sandwich, and soup cafe with as good a view as the expensive places; 360/379-0592. The whole complex has the air of a miniature, slapdash, glad-to-have-you-aboard Fort Worden. It's at the end of Water Street; 800/826-3854 or 360/622-5033.

*"With Water Street considered not only rowdy, but dangerous, the wives and daughters of Port Townsend's more respectable families were drawn to the emerging Uptown business district that offered groceries, soft goods, and protection from downtown riffraff."—Peter Simpson and James Hermanson, in* **Port Townsend: Years That Are Gone.**

***Chevy Chase: Golf and Cabins.*** Golfers have been attracted to this beautiful course since the 1920s. It's been even more of a draw since the "Forest Nine" holes were added in 1997, where you play your way through woodlands and wetlands. Have a golfing binge and stay a few days at one of the four rustic cabins that perch on the bluff. Three have kitchens, and the fourth has a refrigerator and coffeemaker. Nearby are tennis courts, a heated pool, and access to the beach. For golfing or lodging information, call Chevy Chase, 3710 S Discovery Road, Port Townsend; 800/385-8722 or 360/385-0704; chevygolf@aol.com.

***Underground Eatery.*** Descend the stairs to a tunnel-like cavern where, according to unreliable myth, Chinese laborers were smuggled in Port Townsend's lurid past. Here in the Cellars Market (940 Water Street; 360/385-7088) Randy Unbedacht offers lunchtime fare including salads (try the crunchy pea and peanut), sandwiches, homemade soups, and lasagne or quiche by the slice. There's espresso too, and homemade fudge in the candy shop and locally produced art on the walls.

## RESTAURANTS

### BELMONT ★★

In a town where good seafood is almost ho-hum, the Belmont is a special treasure. And in a town where sweeping water views are as common as seagulls, the Belmont stands out. The ideal place to be seated in this three-level restaurant is up the stairs to the back or out on the deck overlooking the bay. And the ideal dish to order is an exquisite fillet of Northwest salmon, broiled exactly right. Taking further advantage of the availability of impeccably fresh seafood, chef Bill Severin offers an appetizer of sushi. Excellent lunch salads include a very large and distinctively Asian-influenced chicken salad. Ask about staying in one of the renovated Victorian-era hotel rooms (two overlook the water). *925 Water St, Port Townsend; center of town, waterside; 360/385-3007; $$; AE, DC, MC, V; local checks only; lunch, dinner every day; full bar.*

***Choice new films and vintage classics draw cinema buffs to the small, elegant Rose Theatre (235 Taylor Street; 360/385-1089), restored by Rocky Friedman to its turn-of-the-century sparkle.***

### BLACKBERRIES ★

This unpretentious little restaurant overlooking the Fort Worden Parade Ground prides itself on its Northwest cuisine, with fresh local produce and seafood and an exemplary vegetarian selection. The dining room is as fresh as a sun porch with Adirondack-style touches—artist Martha Worthley's lovely stenciled walls and curtains (crows and blackberry vines) and twig-framed historic photographs. The Malaysian chicken is spicy and satisfying; cool off with a dollop of ice cream on your blackberry pie. Eat here and feel you're doing your bit to serve the community; all profits from Blackberries go to assist Port Townsend's Community Action programs. *200 Battery Way, Building 210, Port Townsend; Fort Worden State Park Conference Center, 1 mile north of downtown; 360/385-9950; $$; MC, V; checks OK; lunch and dinner Wed–Sat, lunch Sun, May to mid-Sept; beer and wine.*

***Free noontime concerts on summer Fridays take place at Franklin Court in downtown Port Townsend; performers are often participants in Centrum workshops.***

### COHO CAFE ★

It's a favorite place to wake up, and no wonder: the coffee is strong and refills are free, sun streams through the old storefront windows, walls are warmly painted deep orange with a dark purple ceiling, and tables are playfully set with mismatched silverware, bandanna napkins, and fresh flowers. Healthy breakfasts are served all day: homemade seafood sausage, or chunks of smoked salmon, spuds, and red onions in the salmon hash. French toast is soaked in a hazelnut egg custard and served with yogurt and bananas. Toss it down with freshly squeezed juice combos or smoothies with a dose of spirulina, bee pollen, ginseng, ginger, or

***Have a walkabout: Port Townsend's colorful past comes vividly alive when you take a Port Townsend Guided Historical Sidewalk Tour; 360/385-1967.***

wheat grass, and blast into the day. There are lunches too, with miso-based soups and lots of veggies. *1044 Lawrence St, Port Townsend; uptown, across from Uptown Theater; breakfast, 360/379-1030; $; no credit cards; checks OK; lunch Wed–Sun; no alcohol.*

### FOUNTAIN CAFE ★

Some grouchy locals complain about the service, the sauces, and even the paint, but they still bring their out-of-town guests here. And they come in droves, crowding the door of this tiny storefront dining room to inspect the art on the spring-green walls while waiting for a table. The old favorites are still on the menu, including the vegetarian pasta with artichokes, olives, and feta that's been featured for more than ten years. The dinner salad is an impressive heap of fresh field greens on a platter (a big improvement); the wine list is short but includes some good selections. Save room for the loganberry fool, a wondrous blend of custard, fruit, and whipped cream. *920 Washington St, Port Townsend; at foot of Haller Fountain steps; 360/385-1364; $$; MC, V; checks OK; lunch, dinner every day; beer and wine.*

### KHU LARB THAI ★

The gracious service and muted cool greens of the serene decor are a welcome balance to the tingling heat and vibrant flavors that unmistakably identify the food as Thai. One of the best of the aromatic curries is a gently steamed salmon fillet with cabbage and a slightly sweet but still spicy sauce. Delicious chicken wings stuffed with ground pork and shrimp look like fat, crisp lollipops, with a liberal use of pineapple. There's now a sister restaurant in Sequim (see review). *225 Adams St, Port Townsend; off Water St; 360/385-5023; $$; MC, V; local checks only; lunch, dinner every day; beer and wine.*

### LANZA'S ★★

Lanza family recipes are lovingly prepared and proudly served by Lori Lanza and Steve Knight in this uptown Italian restaurant that Port Townsendites voted best for pasta. Choice offerings include homemade sausage, gnocchi, and big calzones stuffed with smoked salmon, fat prawns, and pesto. As always, organically grown local herbs and vegetables are used. Pizza can be ordered to go. There's live music on Friday and Saturday nights. *1020 Lawrence St, Port Townsend; in upper town, above bluffs; 360/379-1900; $$; MC, V; checks OK; dinner Mon–Sat; beer and wine.*

### LONNY'S RESTAURANT ★★★

Lonny Ritter, who has opened some of the Olympic Peninsula's best restaurants, and partner Tim Roth of Seattle fame preside over this exceptional establishment near the boat haven. The soothing decor (warmly tinted walls, graceful arches, and 17th-century botanical prints) and the informed and unpushy waitstaff prepare you for something wonderful. The signature dish of the film *Big Night,* timpano, a huge creation with layers of meats and cooked eggs wrapped in a rich crust and slowly baked, is frequently served as a special appetizer. Other nights, you might have a large, meaty portobello mushroom, fire-grilled and served with roasted tomato and herb oil. If you're used to a low-fat, salt-free diet, forget about it for once and try the oyster stew, made with sweet cream, fennel, and diced pancetta; or the Dungeness crab and mushrooms bathed in cream and imported Italian Gorgonzola. *2330 Washington St (adjacent to Port Townsend Boat Haven), Port Townsend; 360/385-0700; $$; MC, V; checks OK; dinner Wed–Mon; beer and wine.*

### THE PUBLIC HOUSE ★

The Public House is a large space with soaring ceilings, brought into human scale by clever interior design. It's both comfortable (with antique light fixtures, wood floors, dark green wainscoting, and a bar that's a marvel of the cabinetmaker's art) and casual (a great place for a big spicy bowl of gumbo, a Vermont cheddar burger, or a salmon, black bean, and goat-cheese burrito with a light cucumber salsa). Select a beer from the impressive list of drafts and watch the world go by through the big front windows. There's live music at night. *1038 Water St, Port Townsend; on north side of street; 360/385-9708; $; AE, DIS, MC, V; local checks only; lunch, dinner every day; full bar.* ♿

***Port Townsend boasts at least 16 B&Bs, 6 conventional motels, a dozen private getaways (cabins, cottages, and lofts), and 6 Victorian hotels. But don't dare come without a reservation. "In the summer it's not uncommon for the last Saturday-night room in Port Townsend to be gone at noon Friday," they'll tell you at the Chamber of Commerce Visitor Center.***

## SALAL CAFE ★

Breakfasts are justly famous here, with a couple of morning newspapers circulating and locals trading stories back in the solarium. The omelets are legendary, both in quality and in variety (we like the Greek, with basil, spinach, and feta). Other morning starters, such as an oyster scramble or wild salmon frittata, are equally satisfying. Steer clear of pancakes and crepes, which tend toward the doughy and heavy. The lunch menu usually has a pasta or so, and a man-sized meat-loaf sandwich; you may order steak for dinner (for breakfast too, for that matter), or for a true Northwest treat, the mussels tenderly steamed in miso, garlic, and ginger. *634 Water St, Port Townsend; at Quincy; 360/385-6532; $; MC, V; checks OK; breakfast, lunch, dinner every day; beer and wine.* ♿

## SILVERWATER CAFE ★

Owners David and Alison Hero—he's a carpenter, potter, and baker, while she's a gardener and cook—have created the restaurant of their dreams on the first floor of the town's historic Elks Club building. It's a warm, lovely gathering place combining 19th-century architecture with satisfying food served on David's handmade plates and a carefully selected wine list. All dinners begin with a basket of fresh rosemary bread. For starters, try the artichoke pâté, fresh sautéed oysters, or a big spinach salad; lunches include filling salmon-salad sandwiches and hearty homemade soups; local raves for dinner are the green-peppercorn steaks, the Amaretto chicken in a tart-and-spicy lemon and curry sauce, and a seafood pasta loaded with prawns and wild mushrooms and doused with brandy. If you time things right, you can come back after the early movie for a piece of David's lemon poppyseed cake and a cup of chamomile tea. *237 Taylor St, Port Townsend; next to Rose Theater; 360/385-6448; $$; MC, V; checks OK; lunch, dinner every day; beer and wine.*

## LODGINGS

### ANN STARRETT MANSION ★★

The most opulent Victorian in Port Townsend, this multi-gabled Queen Anne hybrid was built in 1885 by a local contractor who just had to have himself a home with more of everything than his neighbors had. He succeeded. The spiral stairway, octagonal tower, and "scandalous" ceiling fresco are visually stunning. All rooms are furnished with antiques and have lovely decorative touches—although some guests may find the florid color scheme (appropriate to the rococo decor) a bit unsettling. The Drawing Room (with a claw-foot, tin bathtub) opens to views of the sound and Mount Baker, while the newer, romantic Gable Suite, which occupies the whole third floor, has a skylight (also with a knockout view) and a spacious seating area. Breakfasts are ample. The house is open for public tours from 1pm to 3pm, when any unoccupied bedrooms are cordoned off for viewing (this creates something of a "living museum" atmosphere). Children are welcome. *744 Clay St, Port Townsend; corner of Adams; 800/321-0644 or 360/385-3205; www.starrettmansion.com; $$; AE, DIS, MC, V; checks OK.* ♿

### BAY COTTAGE ★★

Susan Atkins has turned a cluster of cottages on the shore of Discovery Bay into a delightful retreat. The cottages have good stoves and refrigerators, a tasteful mix of antique furniture, and comfy mattresses covered with feather beds. There's direct access to a private sandy beach—marvelous for swimming, bonfires, and beachcombing. Susan stocks the kitchens with basic breakfast necessities, and when the mood strikes she has been known to bake cookies for guests. Each cottage has its own picnic basket, binoculars, and library. The rose garden is an enchantment. It's an ideal retreat for romantics or, as some say, a great girl getaway. No pets. *4346 S Discovery Rd, Port Townsend; 6 miles west of Port Townsend, ½ mile west of Four Corners Grocery; 360/385-2035; www.olympus.net/biz/getaways/BC/index.htm; $$; no credit cards; checks OK.*

***Your B&B might provide you with TV and VCRs, but if not, you may still take in a flick. Port Townsend's only uptown theater is the Uptown Theater, at Lawrence and Polk. Call 360/385-3883 for shows and schedules.***

***Fort Worden's Alexander's Castle, built by a disappointed-in-love Scottish clergyman in 1892, may harbor a friendly ghoul. Local lore has it that the ghost (quite harmless) is sometimes heard in an unused bedroom in the tower. Says Jim Farmer, Fort Worden State Park manager, "We prefer to let people find out for themselves."***

***Above the mythic Town Tavern hides the Waterstreet Hotel (635 Water Street; 360/385-5467). Of the 16 rooms, most have baths, some have lofts, some have kitchens, and a couple of pricier suites have decks with harbor views. Rooms are cozy and have period furnishings. These lodgings were first offered in the '70s as a place for people to drop out and assess their lives; they still welcome any travelers on a budget to drop in and do the same.***

### THE COMMANDER'S GUEST HOUSE

View Coast Guard, Army, and Navy commanders used to live in this two-story home; now it's a bed-and-breakfast on the beach near Point Hudson Resort. The three rooms are generously provided with such amenities as dressers—a rarity in a B&B—large closets, and sitting areas. All have private baths and wonderful views. You choose the venue for breakfast: in the formal dining room, by the living-room fire, or on the porch overlooking lawns and beach. *400 Hudson St, Port Townsend; east end of Water St, follow signs; 888/385-1778 or 360/385-1778; www.waypt.com/commander; $$; no credit cards; checks OK.*

### FORT WORDEN ★

Twenty-four nobly proportioned former officers' quarters, dating to 1904 when Fort Worden was built to guard the entrance to Puget Sound, have been made into spacious lodgings, each with a complete kitchen, at bargain rates (great for family reunions, but there are a few smaller homes for couples, too). The most coveted of the one-bedroom lodgings is Bliss Vista, perched on the bluff, with a fireplace and plenty of romantic appeal. Off by itself, the three-story brick turret called Alexander's Castle, built in the 1890s, looks as though it would be at home on a Scottish moor. Reservations should be made at least a year in advance. *200 Battery Way, Port Townsend; 1 mile north of downtown, in Fort Worden State Park; 360/385-4730; $$; no credit cards; checks OK.*

### HASTINGS HOUSE/OLD CONSULATE INN ★★

This ornately turreted red Victorian on the hill is one of the most frequently photographed of Port Townsend's "Painted Ladies." It is also one of its most comfortable. All of the immaculate rooms have closet-size private baths, but guests in the enormous Master Suite can soak in a claw-foot bathtub, later warming themselves in front of their own antique fireplace. The third-floor Tower Suite, with a sweeping bay view and swathed in lace, is the essence of a Victorian-style romantic valentine. There's also a hot tub for guest use. Owners Rob and Joanna Jackson won't let anyone go hungry:

rates include afternoon tea, evening desserts and cordials—and next day, a mammoth seven-course breakfast, over which Joanna is more than delighted to wittily recount the inn's history. *313 Walker St, Port Townsend; on the bluff, at Washington; 800/300-6753 or 360/385-6753; www.oldconsulateinn.com; $$$; AE, MC, V; checks OK.*

### HERITAGE HOUSE ★

View Visitors to this hillcrest Victorian bed and breakfast find a sprightly variety of refinished antiques, complementing guest rooms with names like Lilac and Morning Glory. Five of the seven rooms have private baths; the Peach Blossom has an oak-and-tin claw-foot bathtub that folds away when not in use. Relax in the evenings on the porch swing; in the mornings, perhaps, over a breakfast of decadent French toast. The views over the north sound and the business district rival those of Heritage's venerable neighbor, the James House. Children over 8 years are permitted, but pets are not. *305 Pierce St, Port Townsend; corner of Washington; 800/385-6867 or 360/385-6800; $$; AE, MC, V; checks OK.* ♿

### THE JAMES HOUSE ★★★

View The 110-year-old James House, first bed and breakfast in the Northwest (since 1973), is still in great shape, though when a gale blows off the strait and hits the high bluff, you are glad to be in one of the three rooms that have a fireplace or a wood-burning stove. This fine B&B rests in the competent hands of Carol McGough, who is still improving it, continually freshening the 12 rooms and the delightful garden. Rooms in the front of the house have the best views across the water. All but two rooms have private baths, but the shared facilities are spacious and well equipped. The main floor offers two comfortable parlors, each with a fireplace and plenty of reading material. Breakfast is served either at the big dining room table or in the kitchen with its antique cookstove. The bungalow on the bluff is a special place, with the same view as the main house and its own garden sitting area. Children over 12 welcome. *1238 Washington St, Port Townsend; corner of Harrison; 800/385-1238 or*

*360/385-1238; info@jameshouse.com; www.jameshouse.com; $$; AE, MC, V; checks OK.*

### LIZZIE'S

Lizzie, the wife of a tugboat captain, put the deed of this model of Victorian excess in her own name; her name now also graces a line of bath lotions created by owners Patti and Bill Wickline. Breakfast, served around an old oak table in the cheerful kitchen, can turn into a friendly kaffeeklatsch; a soak in the tub in the black-and-white corner bathroom—especially if the sun is slanting in—is a neo-Victorian treat. There are views from several of the seven bedrooms, all of which have private baths and flowered decor. Lizzie's Room comes with its own fireplace. Two parlors seem to have been plucked from the past; in one you'll even find a vintage stereoscope. *731 Pierce St, Port Townsend; near corner of Lincoln; 800/700-4168 or 360/385-4168; www.kolke.com/lizzies; $$; DC, MC, V; checks OK.*

### MANRESA CASTLE

Inspired by German castles on the Rhine, Port Townsend's first mayor—an immigrant from Prussia—built his citadel of a mansion on the city's highest point in 1892. After various transmutations it became a guest house in 1970, and continues to dominate the skyline. The views are high, wide, and handsome, especially from the Tower Suite in the turret. Forty rooms open off long halls running the length of the building; each has private bath, cable TV, phone, and Victorian furnishings. Continental breakfast is included. The Victorian Restaurant is open to the public for dinner every night in summer, Wednesday–Saturday in winter; brunch is served Sunday mornings. The Edwardian Cocktail Lounge, in what was once the mayor's elegant parlor, is still quite elegant, and offers a sweeping view of the bay as well as a respectable wine list. Drinks are dispensed from a historic bar that once graced the Savoy Hotel in San Francisco. *7th and Sheridan, PO Box 564, Port Townsend; north of Sims Way (Hwy 20) on Sheridan, southeast corner of 7th and Sheridan; 800/732-1281 or 360/385-5750; www.manresacastle.com; $$; DIS, MC, V; checks OK.*

### PALACE HOTEL ★

The 1889 Romanesque-style Palace places visitors in the midst of Port Townsend's shopping and gawking district. The 15 rooms retain the building's ex-bordello atmosphere; Marie's Room (she was the durable madame of the house until the mid-1930s) is decorated in the same burgundy and forest green that it sported in the 1890s. Some rooms have kitchenettes. Warning: Long flights of stairs, though handsome reminders of another era, can be a challenge, and nightlife noises from a nearby tavern can make for a restless sleep. Still, it's worth a venture. Continental breakfast is brought to your room, and off-street parking is available. *1004 Water St, Port Townsend; corner of Tyler; 800/962-0741 or 360/385-0773; palace@olympus.net; www.olympus.net/palace; $$; AE, DIS, MC, V; checks OK.*

### QUIMPER INN ★★

The light from all the windows plays across richly hued walls, suffusing every corner of the house with a mellow glow. A first-floor bedroom resembles a library with a comfortable bed and bath, and upstairs there is a lovely suite with period decor and private bath. The room with bay windows and a brass bed also has its own commodious bath with a 6-foot-long tub, a pedestal sink, and wicker furniture. Two rooms share baths. Sue and Ron Ramage treat their inn and their guests with thoughtful care. Breakfasts are well executed. They'll lend you a mountain bike, or pack you a picnic basket. *1306 Franklin St, Port Townsend; corner of Harrison; 800/557-1060 or 360/385-1060; www.olympus.net/biz/quimper/quimper.html; $$; MC, V; checks OK.*

### RAVENSCROFT INN ★

A nonconformist among the surrounding Victorians, Ravenscroft Inn was built in 1987, with a design borrowed from historic South Carolina. The structure is large and impressive, with a long front porch, redwood-stained clapboards, and a graceful end chimney. A suite on the third floor sports dormer windows that overlook the town and harbor. Thick, warm carpeting throughout the house deadens sound and creates immediate coziness. The color scheme in every room is unique; each has wicker or antique-reproduction furniture and custom upholstery, and one romantic room on the second floor has its own fireplace. Sometimes breakfast, served in the immense open-style kitchen, comes with a piano accompaniment. *533 Quincy St, Port Townsend; on the bluff, at Clay; 800/782-2691 or 360/385-2784; ravenscroft@olympus.net; www.ravenscroft.com; $$; AE, DC, DIS, MC, V; checks OK.*

# NORTHERN SHORE

The Strait of Juan de Fuca, the primary access by sea to the Pacific Northwest, is a broad and busy international waterway that marks the northern boundary of the Olympic Peninsula. Across the water to the north, Canada's Vancouver Island and the city of Victoria are plainly visible. To the south the jagged peaks of the Olympic Mountains define the horizon. The towns, shops, and billboards along Highway 101 diminish after you branch off to Highway 112, just past Port Angeles. Along the way, travelers find a range of intriguing opportunities, from a voyage "abroad" on the Victoria ferry to a wilderness hike into Olympic National Park.

*If bird-watching's the nation's second-most popular hobby, fishing's not far behind, says Tommy Thompson, whose Greywolf Angler occupies one end of Wild Birds Unlimited in Gardiner (275953 Highway 101 East; 360/797-7177; greywolf@olympus.net; www.clallam.com/greywolfangler). For fly fishers, including neophytes, he purveys supplies and tips (gleaned from his lifetime as a wielder of the rod), and in fall and spring teaches fly tying.*

## ACTIVITIES

***Whistle Stop.*** You can't miss the row of colorful cabooses as you round Discovery Bay on Highway 101. They look like giant toys, and kids clamor to stop. This is Railroad Park (282023 Highway 101 East; 360/385-9490). The cabooses are lined up on the old rail line that ran from Port Angeles to Port Townsend. In the first, 16 flavors of ice cream are on display. In the Candy Depot, choose from 120 different candies and a wide variety of chocolates and truffles. The deli caboose offers soft drinks, pizza by the slice, salads, sandwiches, and espresso. Pull a handle and hear an old-time train whistle, then settle at a table outside for a snack with a bay view.

***Birds by the Way.*** At Gardiner, Birds Unlimited (275953 Highway 101; 360/797-7100; wildbird@olympus.net) has built its nest, a convenient journey-break between Port Townsend and Sequim. There's plenty here for both avid birders and those who don't know a finch from a flamingo: binoculars, bird calls, feeders, seed, dozens of styles of birdhouses, books, birdbaths—and a chance to listen to a recording of the songs or sounds of the bird of your choice. Outside, a gazebo and benches in the flower garden command a view of Discovery Bay. Grab an espresso and sit quietly to watch the wild birds that flock to the feeders.

***Fun & Games.*** At the head of Sequim Bay at Blyn, bright lights and crammed parking lots alert you to the 7 Cedars

Casino (270756 Highway 101, Sequim; 800/4LUCKY7 or 360/683-7777; 7cedars@olympus.net), an enterprise of the Jamestown S'Klallam tribe. Its timbered facade, like a row of giant longhouses, is fronted by massive totem poles carved by artist Dale Faulstich. Inside are spacious gaming rooms, but one need not be a gambler to come here. Stop for lunch or dinner at the Salish Room (a great seafood buffet Friday and Saturday nights). The Totem Lounge serves the best $4.95 steak dinner in town, all day every day. Or get a snack at the Bingo Bay Deli. Take in live entertainment, dance, and in the gift shop view samples of the stunning artwork available in the Northwest Native Expressions Gallery in the tribal headquarters across the road (1033 Old Blyn Highway; 360/681-4640). Awesome masks, framed artwork in varied media, and silver jewelry inspired by native lore are displayed. You could spend $5,000 on a bentwood box or $50 on a spirit stone. The casino has free shuttle service from Port Angeles, Sequim, and Port Townsend, and limos for hire. Open daily at noon.

***Get a boater's-eye view of the birds from the* Miss Pat*, a tour boat that operates from John Wayne Marina (2577 W Sequim Bay Rd; 360/683-6521). Captain Fred will cruise where you choose: to Protection Island, Discovery Bay, or past the lighthouse at the end of the Dungeness Spit.***

***The Duke's Marina.*** Long ago, John Wayne anchored his *Wild Goose* in Sequim Bay and envisioned a marina. He donated land to the Port of Port Angeles and the dream came true, though posthumously. Today John Wayne Marina has slips for 300 boats, picnic tables, waterside walks, a restaurant, trailer parking, and rest rooms with showers. It's a prime waterfowl-watching spot, especially in fall and winter, when grebes, loons, and scoters paddle about in the bay. Take Whitefeather Way from Highway 101, driving a scant half mile on W Sequim Bay Road; 2577 W Sequim Bay Road; 360/683-9898.

***Camp the Bay.*** Wooded Sequim Bay State Park, just south of John Wayne Marina, offers picnic areas, rest rooms, pay phones, hiking trails, kitchens, facilities for the disabled, and 86 car and RV campsites plus 3 for hikers and bikers. With its 1,000-foot beach, boat launch, and moorage, it's a popular spot for fishing, scuba diving, clamming and oystering (when safe—check the state hotline, 800/562-5632), and crabbing. It's open year-round, and fills up fast in the summer, especially the choice campsites by the beach. Reserve by calling 800/452-5687.

## SEQUIM

*Stop at Sequim's east border, where the Chamber of Commerce information center (1192 E Washington; 360/683-6197) has pointers on parks, lodgings, and things to do. Open daily.*

Although the name Sequim (pronounced Skwim) means "Quiet Waters," it's the driest place in Western Washington, thanks to the rain shadow cast by the Olympic Mountains to the southwest. This climatic oddity brought retirees and others looking for a place in the sun. Now there are fewer hayfields and more new homes, and more motels and fast-food places along the highway. But it's still a friendly little town blessed with striking views of the mountains and the Strait of Juan de Fuca. The annual Irrigation Festival, celebrating the date over a century ago when water was first turned on in the irrigation ditches, testifies to the Sequim–Dungeness Valley's dependence, still, on water to keep things green. Take a side trip from Highway 101, which was relocated in 1999 to bypass Sequim, and you'll find that Washington Street, no longer clogged with traffic, has become more like the small-town main street it used to be. Sequim lures the traveler with flower baskets on lampposts, murals, pocket parks, benches and, on summer Saturdays, a lively farmers market (2nd and Cedar), where on special occasions the spirited Sequimarimba band performs.

## ACTIVITIES

***Lavender Land.*** Sequim decided a few years ago to become Lavender Capital of the Western World, and it just might happen. The annual midsummer Lavender Festival includes walk-throughs and U-picks at the valley's half-dozen lavender farms, sales of dozens of varieties of plants, demonstrations of crafts like making lavender wands and sachets, sampling lavender snacks from cookies to sorbets, or sipping a lavender margarita; 360/683-5774.

***Herbal Persuasion.*** After savoring the rows of fragrant herbs and beds of lavender at Cedarbrook Herb Farm, you'll be a pushover for the dozens of varieties of plants for sale. In the gift shop inside the historic farmhouse, Terry Anderson answers questions about the nurture of your purchases and sells dried flowers, potpourri, herb cookbooks, herb vinegars, garlic braids, and baskets for every occasion. Open daily; 1345 Sequim Avenue S; 2 blocks south of Highway 101; 360/683-7733.

***It's the Berries.*** June and July are U-pick time: Cameron's Berry Farm (699 Hendrickson Road; 360/683-6765) for strawberries and Graysmarsh Farm (1339 Woodcock Road; 360/683-5563) for strawberries and, a bit later, raspberries. Graysmarsh also sells luscious berry jams. In August the picking's free along rural roads if you're willing to risk the thorns of the wild Himalaya brambles, loaded with big juicy berries.

***Local Lore.*** Rainshadow Books 'n More (609 W Washington Street, Sequim; 360/681-0300; rainshadowbks@tenforward.com) is your best bet for local and regional guidebooks, travel books, and works by local authors. A special play-puzzle-reading area is lined with walls of children's books and has tables and child-sized chairs for young readers.

***Elements Cafe.*** This skylit, cheerful room at the back of the Olde Sequim Market Place (126 E Washington; 360/681-5060) with its lightsome, tea-roomy atmosphere nevertheless has a serious side. Chef Steven Shattuck is firm about grease-free cooking, eschews the frying pan, and bakes most everything. Continental breakfast is a bargain with its big plate of fresh fruit, fluffy muffins or scones, and fruit butters. Brunch, lunch, and teatime menus include soups, quiches, sandwiches, salads, and fresh-baked pies, with tea and espresso always flowing.

***Says Catherine Beebe, of the Olympic Game Farm: "Some of the city kids who come here have never even seen a chicken before, let alone a goat or lamb. For them, petting a baby animal is a wonderful personal experience."***

***Animal Farm.*** Tour Sequim's number-one attraction, the 93-acre Olympic Game Farm, founded 53 years ago by Lloyd and Catherine Beebe. Get acquainted with 56 species of animals, from bison to bears, including such movie stars as Charlie the Lonesome Cougar. There's a snack bar, gift shop, a petting area for the kids, and a U-fish pond during summer. The park is open daily from 9am, year-round. In summer there are guided walking tours, and year-round you may drive yourself on sign-guided tours. Along the drive-tour route, at the top of the bluff where the llamas and zebras roam, have a picnic and climb up the observation tower for a wide-open view across the broad valley to the mountains (1423 Ward Road, Sequim; 360/683-4295; www.olygamefarm.com).

***Tusk Tusk.*** The Museum and Arts Center (175 W Cedar; 360/683-8110) is proud to display the 12,000-year-old

Manis Mastodon, or what's left of its skeleton, including a pair of gigantic tusks. It was discovered in 1977 in a marshy field south of Sequim, and a spear point in the creature's rib cage proves the presence of man here much earlier than had been believed. The museum's historical displays will lead you all the way from then to now. The gift shop has a good selection of local history books and unusual Native American artworks. The center is open daily.

***Dungeness Spit.*** One of the state's best hikes is out the Dungeness Spit to the lighthouse (11 miles round-trip). Take Voice of America Road from Lotzgesell Road and drive through the Dungeness Recreation Area campground to the trailhead. The tramp begins with a forest trail, then it's down to the sandy, gravelly spit, with its backbone of silvery driftwood. Hiking is easiest at low tide. Some 250 species of birds have been recorded here. In the bay, look for scoters, brant, loons, American wigeon, mallards, and great blue herons. In the treetops, maybe a bald eagle. On the seaward side, murres, grebes, oldsquaws, and cormorants ride the swells. Clamming and fishing (with appropriate licenses) are permitted; oystering is not. Horseback riding is permitted on designated weekdays. The lighthouse is automated now, but members of the local chapter of the U.S. Lighthouse Society staff it and offer tours. Remember that the whole spit is a wildlife refuge, and birds come first. Visitors should avoid areas that are off-limits, and obey the rules: no pets, beach fires, jogging, Frisbees, hunting, vehicles, kites, driftwood collecting, or camping. But the county campground on the uplands above the spit is one of the peninsula's nicest, with trees and shrubs affording privacy to the 65 sites. It's open summer only, no reservations; 360/683-5847. Information on the Dungeness National Wildlife Refuge, including what birds to look for, is available from the U.S. Fish and Wildlife Service (about halfway between Sequim and Port Angeles; 33 S Barr Road, Port Angeles; 360/457-8451). There's a $3 fee per family to enter the refuge, which is open daily year-round, dawn to dusk.

***Bird-watching on the spit is best from September to May, when waterfowl and shorebirds begin their flights to northern climes. But harbor seals still pop their heads up to say hello in summer, and you might even see a pod of orcas on the seaward side.***

***Seafood Sources.*** Devotees of Dungeness crab swear by Macomber Seafoods (825 W Washington; 360/683-4716), which also has some of the freshest oysters around. Dungeness crab, other seafood, and nautical gifts are available at the Sea

***North of Sequim, a stroll through history starts with the Old Dungeness Schoolhouse on Sequim-Dungeness Way at Towne Road, an impeccably maintained 108-year-old school that's now a community center. A walk along the main street of tiny Dungeness takes you past many a weathered house that dates to the turn of the century. Next to the Three Crabs Restaurant, rows of pilings stretch out into the water, each one like as not serving as perch for a gull. This is all that's left of a 4,000-foot dock where ocean-going ships tied up a century ago.***

Shop and Crab Shack, next to the Three Crabs Restaurant (11 Three Crabs Road; 360/683-4809).

***Railroad Bridge Park.*** This family-friendly park on the Dungeness River centers on a historic railroad bridge, now rebuilt and as sturdy as it was when trains thundered over it 80 years ago. Hiking, horse, and biking trails, a picnic shelter, interpretive signs about the wildlife and the river, and great perches for fishing and bird-watching make this a rare outdoor recreation spot only a mile from busy Highway 101. A Dungeness River Natural History Center is under construction at the east end of the bridge. Take Priest Road north from Washington Street, west of town, then turn left on Hendrickson Road and go to the end; 360/681-8060; www.dungenessrivercenter.org.

***Farm Bounty.*** Nothing's fresher than the produce or more helpful than the help at Sunny Farms (261461 Highway 101 W; 360/683-8003; just west of the Dungeness River bridge.) Cukes, corn, melons, and more come from nearby fields, and the farm offers a wide range of organically grown fruits and vegetables. The deli makes sandwiches to your specifications. The array of teas, herbs, spices, pasta, and grains is stupendous. Open daily.

***Go for Golf.*** So far, the Sequim-Port Angeles area has one public golf course, though another is in the works. The Dungeness Golf & Country Club (1965 Woodcock Road, Sequim; 800/447-6826 or 360/683-6344) has a creek on the back nine, great mountain views, and a restaurant and cocktail lounge. For golfers dedicated to perfecting their game, the Parfect Golf Center and Driving Range (corner of Highway 101 and S Boyce Road, Sequim; 360/681-5228) offers a covered, lighted, heated driving range; lessons; and junior programs.

## RESTAURANTS

### ECLIPSE

Tom Wells, a former physicist and perennial eclipse nut, is this modest-sized restaurant's co-owner, host, and sole waiter. Whenever an eclipse is due, anywhere in the world, he's likely to take off, to heck with the clientele. When open, the restaurant starts serving the creations of Cambodianborn Lay Yin, Tom's wife, at 8am and closes by 3pm, and many or all of the dishes may disappear even before noon. (In-the-know locals phone ahead and have Yin set aside their order.) Diners enter through the back door of the remodeled tract home, sit at a minuscule counter or at one of the two tables, and consider themselves blessed to eat whatever is available from the predominantly Southeast Asian menu: chicken congee, a thick rice soup (and breakfast favorite), or that universal snack, the spring roll—here delicate and delicious. Group dinners, with 20 or more dishes, can be arranged. *139 W Alder Street, Sequim; 3 blocks north of Washington St, corner of 3rd and W Alder; 360/683-2760; $; no credit cards; checks OK; breakfast and lunch Sat–Tues; no alcohol.*

***From breakfast through lunch, rain or shine, the Sunshine Cafe (135 W Washington Street; 360/683-7445) glows with good feeling and buzzes with chat. The tiny eatery is favored by locals, who almost have assigned seats. Service is quick and cheery, food is home-cooked and dependably good, and the check won't make much of a dent in your pocketbook. Open seven days.***

### HIWAY 101 DINER

Welcome to the Hiway 101 Diner, which may have to change its name since 101 moved south. It's a neon-lit, nostalgia-driven place where the back end of a 1956 T-bird serves as a jukebox, playing old Hit Parade songs. You can sit in a booth with sweet June Allyson smiling down on you, listen to "Two to Tango," and wrap your fist around a juicy Awful Awful Burger. Expect the usual diner food at breakfast; it's the burger-and-pizza offerings that have the edge here, as well as the skillfully seasoned clam chowder—the winner in the peninsula's 1995 Clam Chowder Cook-off. *392 W Washington St, Sequim; 360/683-3388; $; MC, V; checks OK; breakfast, lunch, dinner every day; no alcohol.*

### JEAN'S DELI ☆

Jean Klahn moved her popular deli cafe from an old corner minimart west of Sequim into a wonderfully renovated 104-year-old church in the heart of town, and the faithful are giving thanks. Breakfast (which starts at 6) still features the famous honey buns and fresh-baked bagels; soups and sandwiches are as delightful as ever. So are the carrot cake and "lemon lush" desserts. *134 S Second Ave (at Bell), Sequim; 360/683-6727; $; no credit cards; checks OK; breakfast, lunch Mon–Sat; no alcohol.*

### KHU LARB THAI II ★

When this outpost of the admired Port Townsend restaurant opened, Sequim residents rejoiced; no more 30-mile drives to savor the vibrant flavors of Thailand. The building is not much on the outside but inside is prettier, with an elegant rose (the restaurant's namesake) on every table. Newcomers to Thai food should request the tried-and-true *Tum Kah Gai* (a chicken soup with a coconut and lime broth), the *Phad Thai* (sweet, spicy noodles stir-fried with egg, bean cake, and vegetables), or the garlic pork. There's a wide assortment of spicy, aromatic curries, and ample choices for vegetarians. Dinnertimes are often crowded; parties of six or more may reserve. *120 W Bell St, Sequim; 1 block north of Washington St, west of Sequim Ave; 360/681-8550; $; MC, V; checks OK; lunch and dinner Tues–Sun; beer and wine.* ♿

### OAK TABLE CAFE ★

Good, old-fashioned food in bounteous servings is the specialty of this boisterous cafe, owned by a member of the Nagler family (the owners of the Chestnut Cottage and First Street Haven in Port Angeles). Breakfast is a feast of huge omelets, fruit crepes, or the legendary puffy apple pancakes. At lunch, the quiches, sandwiches, soups, and salads are dependably delicious. Service is friendly and efficient, the coffee keeps coming—and the cream is the real thing. *292 W Bell St, Sequim; 1 block south of Washington St at 3rd and Bell; 360/683-2179; $$; no credit cards; checks OK; breakfast every day, lunch Mon–Sat; no alcohol.*

### PETALS GARDEN CAFE ★

A new adjunct to Cedarbrook Herb Farm, Petals perks up the Sequim culinary scene like a breath of rosemary and thyme. A remodeled greenhouse has blossomed as an attractive restaurant, divided into two rooms to add privacy and subtract noise. Lucky chef Pat Allen has but to step out the door to gather herbs, salad greens, and edible flowers from the Cedarbrook gardens. The chicken is free-range, and the organic vegetables are fresh from Sequim farms. The menu blends the flavors of the Mediterranean and Asia (Allen's influences) and Australia (where proprietors

Jim and Bronwyn Salmon hail from). The Tapenades Trilogy dinner starter includes traditional (olive, anchovy, and garlic) and innovative (e.g., Greek skordalia garlic) and is generous enough for two. Follow this with New Zealand beef massaged with a garlic herb rub, and you've tasted the best of two hemispheres. Breakfast and lunch are similarly multicultural: the Ploughman's Lunch is Brit with an Australian accent, and there's a whiff of Cedarbrook mint in the potatoes in the niçoise salad. But high tea is decadent, unadulterated Empress-style. *1345 S Sequim Ave; 2 blocks south of Hwy 101; 360/683-4541; $$; no credit cards; checks OK; breakfast, lunch, and high tea Tues–Sun, dinner Fri–Sat; beer and wine.*

## LODGINGS

### DUNGENESS BAY MOTEL ☆

If you can't decide whether you'd rather look at the Olympics or Dungeness Spit when you wake up, here you get both. The row of neat little cottages, with their appliques of seagulls, has been a familiar sight on the bluff along Sequim's Marine Drive for decades. Units are arranged in pairs with covered carports in between. Five have kitchens, living areas with bedroom alcove, baths with shower, and TV. A larger unit has a fireplace, full kitchen, separate bedroom, and full bath. Furnishings are simple and practical, as befits a place where guests are likely to come tramping in from the beach with a bucket of clams. Owners Karin Koller-Webb and John Webb keep everything trim and shipshape and have all the answers about hiking to the lighthouse, clamming, dining, whatever you need to know. *140 Marine Dr, Sequim; 7½ miles from downtown Sequim on Marine Dr; 888/683-3013 or 360/683-3013; $$; MC, V; checks OK; www.northolympic.com/; dungenessbay@olympus.net.*

***Dungeness Bay Motel, perched on the bluff overlooking the strait and Dungeness Spit, is an agreeable and affordable headquarters for fishing, hunting and beachcombing. All five neat, compact units have kitchens and boast views of mountains, sea, and the lighthouse at the end of the spit winking reassuringly. (140 Marinie Drive, Sequim; 888/683-3013 or 360/683-3013, dungenessbay@olympus.net***

### GREYWOLF INN ☆

On the east side of Sequim, transplanted Southerners Bill and Peggy Melang converted an abandoned farmhouse into a peaceful B&B offering five tasteful guest rooms. Marguerite, the finest, has a fireplace flanked by a wall of books.

The Melangs' hospitality is always evident (especially at the hearty Northwest breakfast, often varied with North Carolina country ham). A small courtyard with an enclosed hot tub is just outside, along with various exercise machines for the more ambitious. A pergola marks the start of the Way of the Wolf nature trail along the wooded hillside, a favorite of bird-watchers. A broad deck on the north affords a restful view of meadows and Sequim Bay. *395 Keeler Rd, Sequim, WA 98382; 1 mile east of Sequim, north of Hwy 101; 800/914-9653 or 360/683-5889; info@greywolf.com; $$; AE, DIS, MC, V; checks OK.*

### GROVELAND COTTAGE ☆

At the turn of the century it was the finest family home in Dungeness, the valley's first settlement; then a mom-and-pop general store; then Simone Nichols arrived to transform the venerable Victorian into a charmingly relaxed country inn, just a half mile from the beach. Four cheerful rooms are upstairs and there's a cottage in the back with views of fields and orchards. Inside, what used to be the country store has become the Great Room, a congenial spot for catered dinners, small meetings, and weddings; guests may relax here in front of the fireplace. The garden, Nichols's passion, is a re-creation of the one that bloomed here in the early 1900s, with the same burbling creek and possibly descendants of the original paddling ducks. The inn fills up in the summer with guests addicted to little luxuries, such as receiving the newspaper and coffee in your room before sitting down to the four-course breakfast. *4861 Sequim-Dungeness Way, Sequim; follow signs from Sequim toward Three Crabs; 800/879-8859 or 360/683-3565; simone@olypen.com; $$; AE, DIS, MC, V; checks OK.*

### JUAN DE FUCA COTTAGES ☆

Five comfortable cottages atop the cliff and overlooking the Strait of Juan de Fuca offer a variety of views and accommodate two to four. All have whirlpool tubs, kitchens, cable TV, and VCRs with a library of movies. The largest, a two-bedroom suite, has a fireplace, a double whirlpool tub, and a double view—water and mountains.

From the gazebo on the front lawn, contemplate the strait with Victoria over the way, and the long ribbon of Dungeness Spit, inviting an exploration. Across the road a short trail leads down to a narrow beach and a launch area suitable for kayaks. *182 Marine Dr, Sequim; 7 miles north of Sequim; 360/683-4433; www.dungeness.com.juandefuca/; $$; DIS, MC, V; checks OK.*

### RANCHO LAMRO

Once home to one of the Sequim-Dungeness Valley's finest dairy herds, this old barn was transformed by Helen Lamoreux Gilchrist into one of the valley's most charming and original B&Bs. It overflows with memorabilia recalling the good old days on the farm. Both rooms have private baths; the more spacious includes a kitchenette, queen bed, double hideabed, baby grand piano, and wood stove—plus a private patio offering a view of the garden, blooming with the handiwork of Fred Gilchrist. The other bedroom, with twins, also has a small patio. Lest you forget who once lived here, cows are everywhere—photos, statuettes, paintings, ceramics. Upstairs in the high-ceilinged former hayloft are a nicely cluttered kitchen, a bar where guests may watch the cook at work (the padded stools were created from milk cans) and in the breakfast-sitting room, a piano, deep leather sofas and chairs, and a round glass breakfast table supported by a huge wagon wheel. A companion wheel makes the chandelier above. At the south end of this capacious room, a serene sunroom with white wicker furniture offers a sublime view of the Olympic Mountains across the valley. Helen's Continental Deluxe breakfast with its amazing array of homemade pastries, breads, jams, and conserves is one of the attractions that keep guests coming back. *1734 Woodcock Rd, Sequim; across from Dungeness Golf and Country Club on Woodcock west of Cays Rd; 360/683-8133; gilchris@olypen.com; $$; no credit cards; checks OK.*

### TOAD HALL

It helps if you're (a) enchanted with *Wind in the Willows* or (b) seeking traditional English hospitality. The inn burgeons with images and reminders of Ratty, Badger, Toad,

***In Agnew, between Sequim and Port Angeles, prowl around and into an intriguing group of little farm- and railroad-oriented museums at Finn Hall Farm (970 Finn Hall Road; 360/452-9156). Inspect a red-white-and-blue 1920s-era caboose, the tiny Agnew Depot Museum, the Udder Museum (an old milk house) and the Browsery Gift Shop. Kids can hang out with the farm animals. Besides running their working farm, owners John and Carmen Jarvis, who put all this together over the years, will take time out to show it off for free, Wednesday to Sunday (by appointment only in off-season).***

and their haunts. But innkeepers Linda and Bruce Clark offer a bounteous English breakfast, a civilized afternoon tea, and cushy comfort along with the whimsy. In Badger's Lair, the honeymoon suite, the ensuite bathroom is oak-paneled and the Jacuzzi accommodates two. All three rooms have sitting areas and views of the Olympics or the sunset across the fields. While savoring their porridge with maple cream, breakfasters look out at the herb garden and the rose arbor and resolve to work off the calories with a go at the croquet court. *12 Jesslyn Ln, Sequim; corner Sequim-Dungeness Way and Jesslyn Ln; 360/681-2534; toadhall@olympus.net; $$; AE, DIS, MC, V; checks OK.*

## PORT ANGELES

Here where the mountains meet the sea, the town is jumping in summer, with travelers heading for the mountains or the ferries, tourists stopping off on their way around the peninsula, and locals busily going about their business, happy that they chose to live here. Port Angeles is on the edge of the rain shadow, so expect a bit more precipitation than in Sequim, 17 miles east. On the other hand, it's closer to skiing at Hurricane Ridge and a primary access point to Olympic National Park. A good place to begin a tour is on the waterfront with a stop at the Port Angeles Chamber of Commerce Visitor Center (121 E Railroad Avenue; 360/452-2363).

***Stop in at the Mombasa Coffee Company (113-A W First St; 360/452-3238) for the best and briskest espresso drinks in town; they custom-roast daily. The pastries are excellent. On fine days, the wide front window is removed and presto, a sidewalk cafe.***

## ACTIVITIES

***City Pier.*** Picnic areas, sunbathing spots, and a wading beach await at the north end of Lincoln Avenue. From the observation tower you can see all the way to Mount Baker to the east and Vancouver Island to the north across the strait. The pier is home to the Arthur D. Feiro Marine Life Center, a partnership project of Port Angeles, Peninsula College, and Olympic Park Institute: a great place to explore tidepools without getting wet. Volunteer naturalists guide children to the touch tank and point out the sea cucumber, just waiting for a tickle. The 80 species here were all collected from local waters. Open daily; 360/417-6254.

SHOPS ***The Landing Mall.*** Just east of the Coho ferry dock is a bulky two-story former wharf, made over to give shelter to fast-food emporia and a frequently changing cast of shops (115 E Railroad Avenue). The Landing is the home of Downriggers Restaurant, with superb views of the strait and its marine activity (115 E Railroad Avenue; 360/452-2700).

***What to do when the wait for the ferry is four hours long? After your car's in line, check with Royal Victoria Tours, who have a kiosk on the sidewalk near the ferry dock. Besides arranging package tours to Victoria, they offer nature tours on the peninsula, including one to Hurricane Ridge that just might fill in the hours of waiting; 888/381-1800 or 360/417-8006.***

***Set Sail for Victoria.*** The Landing is also where you catch the passenger-only, summer-only *Victoria Express;* 360/452-8088 or 800/633-1589 for reservations. Just to the west, the cars, RVs, bikers, and walk-ons line up for the *Coho,* which sails four times a day in summer, twice a day in fall and winter (except January) into Victoria's Inner Harbour; 360/457-4491 for schedules and estimates of waiting time; www.northolympic.com/coho. Waits of several hours to overnight are not unusual in the summer, which is why it's wise to have a Plan B: Leave the car on this side. In Victoria it's easy to get about on foot, by bus, or, more interestingly, by horsedrawn carriage, rickshaw, or one of the little harbor ferries.

***Take a Walk.*** City Pier is the start of the Waterfront Trail. Eastward, a paved trail with benches and interpretive signs explaining birds and wetlands runs about a mile to the old Rayonier Mill. The westward leg is a 4-mile meander (on foot or by car) along the shore, from downtown shops and restaurants, past the marina, and out on Ediz Hook. The whole trail is handicapped-accessible. Railroad Avenue is a great summertime walk; bustling with trippers, bedecked with flower baskets and planters, and lined with several handy cafes.

***On-the-Wall Art.*** A walk around just a few downtown blocks reveals three murals spanning 250 years of history; the one at Waters West Fly Fishing Outfitters (219 Oak, south of Railroad Avenue) shows the Norman #1, a 1903 steam engine that, alas, never reached the rails. A cheerier mural on the south side of the Seafirst Building, Front and Laurel, depicts the streamlined ferry *Kalakala,* which did yeoman duty between Port Angeles and Victoria in the '30s. At First and Laurel a huge mural shows Port Angeles in 1914, busy creating a new downtown by filling in the tidelands with dirt from the hill to the south: *Sluicing the Hogback.*

## A THREE-STOP WINERY TOUR

***Three producers of prize-winning wines on the north shore of the Olympic Peninsula will welcome you for tastings. Lost Mountain Winery, south of Sequim, is worth the trip just for the drive past fields of lavender and hay, up into the forested foothills with their hidden valleys. About a mile west of Sequim on Highway 101, turn south on Taylor Cut-Off Road, then right on Lost Mountain Road; the winery is about 6 miles from Highway 101. It produces a half-dozen or so reds, including the robust Romeo's Blend—formerly Pipa's Blend and renamed to honor the late winemaster Romeo Conca. More sophisticated is the Poesía (a cabernet-merlot blend): each year's label, a work of art in itself, features a verse by a regional poet. The winery's first white was introduced in 1999. Tasting is accompanied by good cheese and home-baked bread. The winery is open every day during the three-week summer Open Winery; call for information, and for off-season appointments (3174 Lost Mountain Road; 360/683-5229; www.lostmountain.com). Olympic Cellars (255410 Highway 101, Port Angeles; 360/452-0160) does its best to fill up a cavernous remodeled barn on Port Angeles's eastern edge. Besides several varietal reds and whites, it offers its specialty Dungeness Red, White, and Rosé. While sipping, browse the big tasting room for oddments from T-shirts to Lopez Larry's piquant mustards. The winery is open daily, year-round. Camaraderie Cellars nestles in the trees with a grand view of the Olympics, just off Highway 101 west of Port Angeles (334 Benson Road; 360/452-4964; corson4@tenforward.com). It claims to be the farthest northwest winery in the country, and produces limited quantities of two Bordeaux varieties: a cabernet sauvignon and a sauvignon blanc. Open by appointment only.***

***Seafood to Go.*** About a mile from the start of the Waterfront Trail, you'll find Hegg and Hegg (801 Marine Drive; 360/457-3344 or 800/435-3474), purveyors of choice Northwest seafoods. They ship gift baskets and packs of canned smoked salmon, shrimp, oysters, and sturgeon all over the world, and have become the northern peninsula's largest UPS shipper. Still, they're happy to take care of the drop-in customer. For a splurge, get or give a whole smoked salmon. Hegg and Hegg also has a shop in the Landing, 360/457-3733, and one at 2830 Highway 101 E, 360/457-1551.

***Ediz Hook.*** The west end of the Waterfront Trail passes the busy complex of the Daishowa America paper mill at the start of Ediz Hook—said to be the second-longest sandspit in the world (after its sister to the east, Dungeness Spit). At the lagoon just before you reach the mill, you might see a cormorant on a piling or a rock, spreading its wings to dry. The hook is a prime waterfowl-viewing spot. Walk, drive, or bicycle 2 miles out, as far as the Coast Guard station. There's no stopping along the road except at a few pull-outs with limited parking spots, picnic tables, and knockout views of the Olympic Mountains.

***The Port Angeles Visitor Center sells more postcards than any other public facility in Washington except the national parks.***

***Stop for a Snack.*** Bonny's Bakery (215 S Lincoln; 360/457-3585), housed in a recycled historic firehouse, is not your basic bread-and-bagel bakery. It's more of a coffeehouse, social club, and mecca for foodies. Bonny and E. J. Kelly offer exquisite pastries, an inventive sandwich menu, and good honest soups. Sit inside or out on the sunny patio and savor a petite baguette with smoked salmon and cream cheese, or a napoleon and cappuccino.

***Oops! Whatever you forgot, you'll likely find it at Swain's (602 E First, Port Angeles; 360/452-2357). A rambling jumble of a store right on Highway 101, it has stuff for fishing, camping, and hiking, plus edibles, wearables, film, and a good-natured staff that pretty much knows where everything is. Open daily.***

***Minimuseum.*** The county historical society has created a stroll-through display in the lobby of the handsome brick colonial Federal Building at First and Oak (its temporary home while awaiting completion of the new museum), conjuring up the days of donkey engines, sailing ships, and one-room schoolhouses, when Port Angeles was young. It's open Monday to Friday; 360/452-2662.

***Onward and Upward.*** Hikers, climbers, and skiers heading into the Olympic Mountains find what they need—from gear to guides—at Olympic Mountaineering (140 W Front Street; 360/452-0240), briskly operated by co-owners Steve Teufert and Jack Ganster. They, and all their guides, are licensed by Olympic National Park. The most popular destination for alpine mountaineers is Mount Olympus, but Steve and Jack will just as cheerfully organize a half-day jaunt to Goblin's

***The Port Angeles Fine Art Center, perched on a hill above the city, occupies an award-winning home surrounded by parklike grounds. Regional and national art is exhibited in an intimate, elegant setting. Open Thursday through Sunday (1203 E Eighth Street; 360/457-3532).***

Gate on the Elwha or set up a family reunion at Camp Handy. Summers are busy, so plan ahead. And trust your guide. "If you're safe, you're going to have fun," says Steve.

***Fine Foodstuffs.*** Can you find anything that isn't good for you in the Country Aire? Not likely. But you'll find plenty of unusual edibles and delicacies. This food shop has a 23-year record of giving the local health-conscious gourmets what they like. Fresh-squeezed juices are a big draw, as are the cheeses. People come in to see what's new, surveying the shelves and counters as though visiting an art gallery. For serious health nuts, there's an adjoining nutrition center (117 E First Street; 360/452-7175).

SHOPS ***Read All About It.*** Port Book and News is a favorite of the literati and the news-hungry. The book selection is broad and deep, and the magazines number 2,000. The *New York Times* and *Wall Street Journal* are always fresh, and the chalkboard in the window displays the date's events in history and a thought-provoking quotation, courtesy of longtime owner Alan Turner (104 E First Street; 360/452-6367, pbnturner@olympus.net).

***Coffee House Restaurant and Gallery.*** Schmooze over a latte, read an alternative newspaper with your soup, or have a relaxed dinner at this dandy downtown spot. You'll find original soups, salads, sandwiches, crepes, seafood and vegetarian dishes, and splendid desserts. Beer and wine, too. The "gallery" has expanded from works of local artists to include easy-to-wear clothing and crafts, all for sale. Occasional live entertainment (you can count on it the first Friday of the month). Breakfast, lunch, and dinner Tuesday through Saturday; breakfast and lunch on Sunday (118 E First Street; 360/452-1459).

## RESTAURANTS

### BELLA ITALIA ☆

Year in, year out, proprietor Neil Conklin serves the best pastas in town (13 varieties), the freshest produce (he's fortunate in supplier Nash Huber, local evangelist of organic produce), and an innovative menu. Residents have voted it best Italian restaurant on the peninsula for three years running. Chef Dave Senters is intrigued by the fresh seafood the peninsula offers and makes the most of it: the lemon-laden salmon Sicilian style is a steady favorite. The bread salad, a meal in itself, could have come straight from Umbria. Conklin has set out to bring uncommon wines to the peninsula, and it takes a book to present his offerings, some 250 by now, including the aristocrats of the Northwest and selections from France, Australia, Spain, and Chile. *117-B E First St, Port Angeles; under the Country Aire between Lincoln and Laurel; 360/457-5442; $$; AE, MC, V; local checks only; lunch for groups by reservation, dinner every day; full bar.*

***The peninsula has many a record-setting big tree, but most are deep in the forest and not easy to find. One that's very visible from much of Port Angeles is the state's second-largest Pacific madrona, at Eighth and Cherry. It's 85 feet high with a 21-foot circumference and a crown spread of 95 feet. (The state's biggest is in Tacoma's Point Defiance Park.)***

## C'EST SI BON ★★

Yes, it *is* good—especially if you're yearning for a leisurely meal of classic pre-nouvelle French cooking with its splendid sauces. While chef Michele Juhasz stirs and sautés in the kitchen, host Norbert Juhasz may regale waiting guests with tales of his musical experiences in France and Hollywood. A big bowl of onion soup, bubbling under a brown crust of cheese, can serve as a meal in itself for those easily sated, particularly when followed by a refreshing salad. Stick to the simpler items, such as the braised lamb, the classic steak au poivre, and the fresh halibut and salmon served in season—you'll hardly go wrong. The chocolate mousse is wickedly rich, and the wine list has good choices for those who aren't. A glassed-in terrace room offers the most privacy, and garden views. *2300 Hwy 101 E, Port Angeles; 4 miles east of Port Angeles on Hwy 101 E; 360/452-8888; $$$; AE, MC, V; local checks only; dinner Tues–Sun; full bar.*

## CHESTNUT COTTAGE ★

Owners Diane Nagler and Ken Nemirow (who also run First Street Haven) are very particular when it comes to quality food and service. It definitely shows. Their Chestnut Cottage is the place to go for an exceptional breakfast in delightful country Victorian-style surroundings just outside of downtown P.A. A custardy apple and walnut French toast is only one of several morning treats; others include Belgian waffles, pancakes, quiches, frittatas, or lemon blintzes drizzled with raspberry purée. On the simpler side, a bowl of porridge and berries will surely satisfy. Or go exotic with a breakfast pizza (ham and eggs on pita). *929 E Front St, Port Angeles; on Hwy 101, east of the center of town; 360/452-8344; $$; DIS, MC, V; checks OK; breakfast, lunch every day; beer and wine.* ♿

### CHIHUAHUA ★

Like small towns all across the country, Port Angeles has its share of Mexican restaurants. A notch or two above most is the Chihuahua—a small, busy spot that specializes in the foods of northern Mexico. Although most of the dishes cater to Tex-Mex tastes, owners Raphael and Juan Hernandez offer other more regional dishes, such as chile Colorado—a comforting pork stew, thick with chiles, herbs, and spices—or *machaca con huevos*—shredded beef scrambled with eggs, onions, and tomatoes. Occasionally, wonderful soups are bubbling away in the kitchen. On Sunday, ask for the menudo, a hearty soup of tender tripe in a well-flavored broth (especially recommended for hangovers). *408 S Lincoln, Port Angeles; 1 block south of old Clallam County Courthouse, between 4th and 5th; 360/452-8174; $; DIS, MC, V; checks OK; lunch, dinner every day; beer and wine.*

### FIRST STREET HAVEN ★

It's just a skinny slot of a restaurant, easily missed among the storefronts if you're not paying attention. The cinnamon rolls are what draw the locals—in addition to the socializing on Saturday or Sunday morning. Fresh and unusual salads with homemade dressings, hearty sandwiches, pastas, and quiche dominate the menu, and the chili is great on a cold winter day. Expertly made espresso and their own coffee blend are fine jump-starters, especially with a fresh blueberry muffin or sour-cream coffee cake. Prices are reasonable, and service is friendly and attentive. *107 E First St, Port Angeles; at Laurel, next to the Toggery; 360/457-0352; $; no credit cards; checks OK; breakfast, lunch Mon–Sat, brunch Sun; no alcohol.*

### THAI PEPPERS ★

A jolly bronze Buddha greets you when you step into this friendly restaurant and the waitstaff are just as cheery. Proprietor Sonthya Iti (formerly of Sequim's Khu Larb Thai) serves authentic Thai food that many claim is the best on the peninsula. Try the butterflies—a seductively seasoned appetizer of wonton wrappers stuffed with cream cheese, crab, and scallions—plenty for two. Or the *Shu see plar*, fish in a rich red curry sauce spiked with coconut milk and basil. A spicy favorite is swimming rama: stir-fried chicken on a bed of spinach and topped with peanut sauce. Bring a highly seasoned meal to a refreshing close with a scoop of ginger-flavored ice cream. Orders to go, too, for tourists on the run for the Coho or the mountains. *229 N Lincoln St; west side of Lincoln, between Front St and Railroad Ave; 360/452-4995; $$; MC, V; checks OK; lunch and dinner Mon–Sat; beer and wine.* ♿

### TOGA'S INTERNATIONAL ★

Ambitious young owner/chef Toga Hertzog trained in the Black Forest—so it's no surprise that his sauerbraten is a hit. But you might be surprised at his "Jagerstein" meal (you cook it yourself at the table on a hot stone, a method derived from the practice of German hunters out in the forest). Creamy-smooth Hungarian mushroom soup, tinged with paprika, will have you licking your bowl. Lamb shanks are a favorite, as are the Dungeness crab cakes with sautéed prawns Provençal. Hertzog makes all his cakes—the standout is chocolate mousse cake with walnuts. The restaurant occupies a onetime family home and still has a family feel to it—Hertzog's wife runs the dining room. *122 W Lauridsen Blvd, Port Angeles; on Hwy 101 just west of Port Angeles; 360/452-1952; $$; MC, V; checks OK; dinner Tues–Sun; beer and wine.* ♿

## LODGINGS

### B.J.'S GARDEN GATE ★

B.J. and Bruce Paton built this sparkling white Victorian and surrounded it with exquisite gardens, and hardly was the gate painted before guests were clamoring to come in. The inn is poised on a bluff east of Port Angeles above the Strait of Juan de Fuca. The five rooms reflect the Patons' love of history (with names like Victoria's Repose and Napoleon's Retreat) and their taste for fine European antiques—the more substantial the better. Rooms are spacious ("Big furniture needs big rooms," says B.J.), most have Jacuzzis, and all have fireplaces and sitting areas for enjoying the view. The Patons have found ingenious ways to coddle guests: pre-breakfast coffee or tea brought to the room, cookies by the turned-down bed, and by request, in-room massages by licensed therapists. The multicourse breakfast features such specialties as a luscious strawberry soup and apple-stuffed sausage. It's served in the elegant dining room with one of the best views in the house: the flower-bordered lawn, the white picket fence with its garden gate, and Victoria across the water. *397 Monterra Dr, Port Angeles; westbound on Old Olympic Hwy, right on Gunn Rd, then left on Monterra Dr to inn sign; 360/452-2322 or 800/880-1332; bjgarden@olypen.com; $$; AE, MC, V; checks OK.*

### DOMAINE MADELEINE ★★★

View New innkeepers Jeri WEinhold and Paul Pollier have taken over from longtime owners Madeleine and John Chambers, but promise no major changes. The setting is still a big draw—the inn sits among tall firs, lawns, and gardens and looks straight out to the Strait of Juan de Fuca. Of the four sleeping areas, the spacious upstairs Ming Suite with its own large balcony and antique Oriental furnishings is the most sought-after. Besides three rooms downstairs, there's a cozy cottage, a favorite of honeymooners. Guests are served a lavish five-course breakfast; after this indulgence a stroll around the inn's lawns and gardens might be called for, with a good chance of spotting browsing deer or an eagle, as well as Victoria across the water. *146 Wildflower Ln, Port Angeles; north of Old Olympic Hwy, off Finn Hall Rd between Sequim and Port Angeles (call for directions); 360/457-4174; domm@olypen.com; www.northolympic.com/dm; $$$; AE, MC, V; checks OK.*

### OLYMPIC LODGE ★

View This Best Western hotel just seems to offer the right combination of comfort and rustic atmosphere to suit Port Angeles—and if you don't have the time to hike the backcountry, just walk the halls to see what you're missing. Sequim photographer Ross Hamilton has a large collection of work on permanent display. The place is built on a large scale, with a big lobby well supplied with seating, and an adjoining breakfast room. The 106 rooms are spacious and well appointed with cherry furniture. Many have views of the mountains. Amenities include a large heated swimming pool and Jacuzzi spa. *140 Del Guzzi Dr, Port Angeles; on Highway 101, east side of Port Angeles; 360/452-2993 or 800/600-2993; $$–$$$; AE, DC, MC, V; no checks.*

### TUDOR INN ★★

View One of the most handsome buildings in town, this completely restored Tudor-style bed-and-breakfast has a country-manor feel, though it's only 12 blocks from the ferry terminal in a quiet residential neighborhood. The inn boasts many fine antiques—some even for sale, on display in the library. Of the five bedrooms, all with mountain or strait views, a favorite is the Country Room, with a balcony, views of mountains and gardens, a fireplace, claw-foot tub, and walls covered with delicate country scenes handpainted by Roberta Audette. Hospitable hosts Jane Glass and her daughter Katy serve a traditional full breakfast with none of the forced conviviality around the dining table that sometimes afflicts other B&Bs. The gardens get prettier every year. Your hosts will gladly provide transportation to and from the ferry dock and arrange for fishing charters, horseback rides, or winter ski packages. *1108 S Oak St, Port Angeles; 11th and Oak; 360/452-3138; info@tudorinn.com; www.tudorinn.com; $$; AE, DIS, MC, V; checks OK.*

# NORTHWEST CORNER

The shoreline along the Strait of Juan de Fuca between Port Angeles and the Pacific is mostly wild and undeveloped, with three little towns punctuating the route: Joyce, Clallam Bay, and Sekiu. Beyond Sekiu, Highway 112 often hugs the coast, offering a scenic bonanza: waves crashing on rocky shores, laden containerships plowing purposefully and silently along the strait, the occasional migrating whale, and the hulking shape of Vancouver Island across the water. By the time you reach Neah Bay, you're surrounded by a land of rockbound ocean beaches and forested slopes checkered with clearcuts. At the end of the road you can view a moving presentation of Native American culture at the Makah Cultural and Research Center. Parks and recreational areas are conveniently spaced along the way, with several easily reached from Joyce, 16 miles west of Port Angeles.

## LODGINGS

### POND MOTEL

Lodgings are fairly scarce along this stretch of Highway 112. Budget-minded travelers often start or break the journey at the Pond Motel. It's set in the trees, with gardens, a picnic area, barbecue, and a pond with waterlilies, ducks, and a wee bridge leading to a wee island. Several of the ten units have pond views; some have kitchens but equipment is minimal. You might do better to drive 10 miles down the road and have your eggs and hashbrowns while you mingle with the locals at Granny's Cafe (Highway 101 at Indian Valley Motel; 360/928-3266). *North side of Hwy 101, west of Port Angeles; 1425 Hwy 101 W, Port Angeles; 360/452-8422; $; MC, V; no checks.*

## JOYCE

There's more to the town of Joyce than meets the eye of the motorist on Highway 112. Besides a tiny museum, there are a couple of creditable eateries, a gas station, and a hundred-year-old general store, which bills itself as the "University of Joyce" and which owner Leonard Pierce says is the oldest continuously operating general store in Washington (50883 Highway 112; 360/928-3568). The floor creaks and wavers, but Pierce reminds you that loggers have been stomping about here for decades. The museum, nearby, is housed in the only log depot the Milwaukee Line ever had. It's free and open weekends in summer.

***Joyce's blackberry frenzy gets intense the first weekend in August, when the annual celebration and parade, Joyce Daze, overwhelms the town and Highway 112. Motorists have to detour, so you might as well stay and listen to the band, prowl the arts-and-crafts booths, and cast your vote for best blackberry pie.***

## ACTIVITIES

***Shoreline Parks.*** Between Port Angeles and Joyce, several parks lie along the shores of the Strait of Juan de Fuca. At Freshwater Bay a small county park has tidepools teeming with starfish, sea anemones, and tiny darting sculpin. Salt Creek Recreation Area offers camping and picnicking, a playground, a kitchen, and a generous stretch of beach. It's the former site of Camp Hayden, assigned to defend the strait during World War II. Wander about the bunkers that once housed big guns. Pillar Point, another county park, has camping and a boat launch favored by kayakers. Whiskey Creek Beach (360/928-3489) is a private park with very rustic housekeeping cabins, a boat ramp, camping spots, fishing holes in the creek for children, and a mile of shoreline where rockhounds have a ball. It's an old-shoe kind of place and devotees of the laid-back life keep coming back year after year. Cabins have woodstoves and propane lights and appliances; no electricity. Bring bedding and linens.

***"Look at that beaded ceiling—you can't get wood like that these days. Old-timers love this town. People come here from all over the country, just for the nostalgia."—Leonard Pierce, owner of the general store in Joyce.***

***Blackberry Daze.*** People come to Joyce just for the blackberries—those little wild ones that make such memorable pies. At the Round Table (50530 Highway 112; 360/928-2080), wild blackberry pie is enthusiastically promoted during the summer berry season. Call and give 24 hours' notice if you want a whole pie.

***See the Trees Grow.*** Twenty miles west of Joyce, Merrill & Ring's Pysht Tree Farm, the state's oldest continuously owned tree farm, is open by appointment on Friday mornings for guided tours of a forestry trail, where you'll learn all about forest management, from planting to harvest to replanting. There's a nice picnic area, too. Tours are $6 for adults, $4 for children and seniors; PO Box 1058, Port Angeles; 800/998-2382 or 360/452-2367.

# CLALLAM BAY AND SEKIU

Salmon fishing has long brought fishermen to Clallam Bay and Sekiu, twin towns on the Strait of Juan de Fuca. Despite short seasons of late, they still come, for bottom fish if not salmon. Whenever there's a salmon season, Sekiu instantly fills with RVers and there's hardly a room to be had. Both towns have easy-to-get-to beaches.

***Divers like Sekiu because the water is clear, the currents are gentle, and sea life is abundant. The Dive Center at Curley's (Box 265, Sekiu, WA 98381; 360/963-2281) supplies air, rentals, sales, and advice.***

## ACTIVITIES

***Exploring.*** Clallam Bay's county park is practically in town. Take the footbridge, a graceful arch that spans the placid Clallam River. Along the riverside trail, settle at a picnic table and watch for a blue heron or a kingfisher. If you head for the beach, you might find an agate. Walking east, near Slip Point Light, look for life in tidepools and for ancient marine fossils. In Sekiu, a bit farther west on 112, get a snack at the Burger Hut, at the end of the main drag. Just beyond is Olson's Resort. Park near here to walk One-Mile Beach, which follows an old railroad right-of-way, with several access points to the sandy shore below; the third trail down is the least steep. Also in Sekiu, pick up an ice cream cone or a latte at Curley's Resort (near Van Riper's), walk along the docks, and let a proud angler show you his catch.

***Charter a Cruise.*** Cruise to view whales, eagles, puffins, and more with Puffin Adventures, run by longtime wildlife tour operator Steve Boothe, a fount of bird lore. His tours range along the strait and the Olympic Coast National Marine Sanctuary. He'll also take you fishing or scuba diving or kayaking in his own ocean kayaks (beginners welcomed). Paddling sites include the rain-forest rivers, Point of the Arches near Shi Shi (you're sure to see sea lions, seabirds, and maybe whales), and Cape Flattery. If you bring your own kayak, Steve will get you to a launching spot and pick you up. His headquarters are at Trettevik's RV Park at Shipwreck Point on Highway 112 (milepost 7); 888/305-2437 or 360/963-2744; puffin@northolympic.com; www.northolympic.com/puffin.

## LODGINGS

### CHITO BEACH RESORT ★

Eight miles west of Clallam Bay on a point jutting into the strait, this delightful little resort offers peace and quiet and all the seaside scenery you could wish, along with considerable charm and a variety of accommodations. The "Big House," facing the west bay, has two bedrooms, a huge living room, and a full kitchen. What with bunks and daybeds, up to a dozen could spread out here and not feel squeezed. The three cottages (one an A-frame with skylit loft) face the east bay and sleep two to four. They have kitchens and private decks, and are so cozy and *gemütlich* that you might be tempted never to stray, which would be a mistake. Besides the close-at-hand outdoor amenities—the bonfire pit and barbecue grills for cookouts and sing-alongs, volleyball and croquet courts—there are beaches to walk, tidepools to investigate, and whales to watch. Bob and Pat Ness, the owners, can point you to whatever outdoor activity you fancy: wildlife cruises, fishing charters, hikes in the Olympics, rain-forest explorations, excursions to nearby Neah Bay and the Makah Museum, or self-guided birdwatching tours between Clallam Bay and Cape Flattery. *7639 Hwy 112, 8 miles west of Clallam Bay; PO Box 270, Clallam Bay; 360/963-2581; chitobch@olypen.com; www.olypen.com/chitobch; $$; no credit cards; checks OK.*

### VAN RIPER'S RESORT

The only waterfront hotel in the area, Van Riper's is a comfortable, family-operated place. The smaller street-side rooms are nothing special, but those facing Clallam Bay can look out at fishing boats moored at the docks, or to the strait and the rugged coastline of Vancouver Island across the way. Two of these units are large apartments (six can sleep comfortably) with complete kitchens, suitable for a family or group of friends. A small house up the hill is also available. Owners Chris and Val Mohr also operate the little store on the premises, offering bait, tackle, and supplies. There's a launch ramp. *280 Front St, Sekiu; corner of Front and Rice on the main street; 360/963-2334; $; MC, V; checks OK.*

***Your best and almost only bet for a meal between Joyce and Neah Bay is the Breakwater Restaurant, on a rise on Highway 112 a couple of miles west of Clallam Bay. You'll find fare several notches above standard, with the occasional surprise like a sweet cabbage soup, and a good fresh salad bar. The restaurant serves breakfast, lunch, and dinner daily. Watch the waves break on the breakwater as you eat; 360/963-2428.***

### WINTERSUMMER INN ★★

From Highway 112 it's just another nice old house in Clallam Bay with no clue as to the magnificent views from the back. When it was remodeled into a bed-and-breakfast (still the only one in Clallam Bay or Sekiu), the owners recognized that the overlook of the Clallam River, the strait, and Vancouver Island was its biggest asset. They built a broad deck off the first floor, jutting out almost over the river, furnished with tables and potted plants and flanked by flower and herb gardens. Stairs lead up to another deck, the private domain of guests in the second-floor apartment, the place to choose for maximum space and seclusion. The apartment's decor is 1950s-family-room, but it has a complete kitchen and, what with trundle beds and hideabeds, cozily sleeps eight. It also has a fireplace and a pool table. The two downstairs rooms are more stylishly furnished; one has a Jacuzzi. Note the art on the walls by local artists, including some striking paintings and works in wood by innkeeper K. C. Winters. She offers easygoing hospitality; you're welcome to use the kitchen, and say kind words to the family dog. Name your time for the ample breakfast, up to 10am. If you ask in advance, K. C. may serve you dinner. *16651 Hwy 112, Clallam Bay; on the right as you leave town westbound; 360/963-2264; $; no credit cards; checks OK.*

***In August, Neah Bay breaks out in Makah Days, a celebration of the granting of citizenship to native people in 1924. It's a three-day event, with a parade, salmon bake, footraces, bone games (Indian gambling), Indian dances, fireworks, and fiercely competitive canoe races in the bay.***

## NEAH BAY

This is literally the end of the road: Highway 112 ends at Neah Bay, home of the Makah Indians for 2,500 years and the only town on their reservation. It's the gateway to a number of off-the-beaten-path activities, at sea or on shore. The harbor is a favored destination for fishermen; the Makah have revitalized their fishing port with the addition of a new jetty, floats, and docks with moorage for 200 boats. It's said to be the only harbor between Port Angeles and San Francisco where you don't have to cross a bar.

### ACTIVITIES

***The Only Store in Town.*** Washburn's General Store, on the left as you come into town (360/645-2211) is bigger and brighter than the old one that burned down a few years ago. A Neah Bay mainstay longer than even some of the elders can remember, it continues as the town's unofficial social center. Stock up here for a camping trip, sit down for a custom-made sandwich in the deli, get your fishing license, buy some boots, and discover a Native art treasure.

***Top off your tour of Neah Bay with your very own salmon bake, in the traditional Makah fashion. Donna Wilkie will put one on for groups of 6 to 30 at her beachfront home, 360/645-2554 or 360/645-2201.***

***Fishing.*** Salmon seasons vary from year to year, but there are other fish in the sea: halibut, cod, and rockfish. Charters are available at Big Salmon Resort, 360/645-2374 or 800/959-2374; Farwest Resort, 360/645-2270; and Raven Charters, 360/645-2121.

***Beaches.*** Hobuck Beach is open for picnics (no fires), surfing, and horseback riding, and has camping and rental cabins in summer; 360/645-2422. Farther on, the Tsoo-Yas (Sooes) Beach is accessible (if you pay the landowners a parking fee). All these areas are on tribal lands, and the Makah expect visitors to help them maintain their unspoiled wilderness character. Shi Shi Beach, within Olympic National Park's coastal strip, is accessible by a 4-mile puddly trail, which the Makah plan to upgrade. Meantime, they permit hikers to use it; you'd be wise to pay to park at one of their nearby spaces before setting out. Shi Shi, one of the park's or indeed the country's most beautiful wild beaches, is a crescent with Portage Head at the north, Point of the Arches at the south—a procession of castle-like sea stacks that head out to sea as though intending to make it to Japan. Sturdy, determined hikers can start here for the beach hike to Cape Alava.

***Someday a coastal trail will reach from Cape Flattery to the Columbia River. The Makah's Cape Flattery Trail and their in-the-works trail connecting tribal lands with Olympic National Park at Shi Shi Beach will form the northern stretch. Information: National Coast Trail Association; 503/335-3876 or www.coast-trails.org.***

***Where to Stay in Neah Bay.*** Besides several plain-and-simple motels that cater to fishermen, there's the decommissioned Air Force station 2 miles west of Neah Bay, now Makah tribal headquarters and with a few rooms for rent in the former enlisted men's quarters. They're little more than dorms, but all have private baths and it beats camping in the rain. Makah Tribal Center; 360/645-3325.

***Hiking.*** The trailhead to Cape Flattery, a rocky, wave-battered headland, is reached by a 5-mile road from the western outskirts of Neah Bay. The Makah have rebuilt the formerly very muddy path; their new walker-friendly half-mile puncheon and boardwalk trail gets you there dry-shod. From the viewing platform atop the sheer cliffs you can see the most northwesterly point in the Lower 48: Tatoosh Island, a half-mile away, with its lonely lighthouse. From the cape, you may sometimes see cow-calf pairs of gray whales migrating northward during April and May.

***The best breakfast-with-a-view in town is at the Makah Maiden Cafe on Bay View Avenue in Neah Bay. Look out at Waadah Island and the long rocky breakwater that protects the harbor and watch soaring eagles searching for their own breakfast. The restaurant serves lunch and dinner too; open daily (1471 Bay View Ave; 360/645-2274).***

***For the Birds.*** Cape Flattery is a famous bird-watching spot, especially during the raptor migration when the big birds gather here to wait for a favorable wind to help them across the strait. A list of 239 winged species that have been spotted near or at the cape is available from the Makah Tribal Planning Office, 360/645-2201, or at the Makah Cultural and Research Center.

***Makah Cultural and Research Center.*** This architecturally striking building, on the left as you enter Neah Bay, was built by the Makah to house artifacts discovered at Ozette Village near Cape Alava. To this world-famous archaeological collection they've added stunning displays depicting their ancestral and whaling traditions. See full-size cedar canoes, a longhouse (with sound effects), dioramas of the seashore accompanied by gulls' cries and sea lions' roars, and hundreds of items reflecting the rich Makah culture. The gift shop has works of Native artists and a good book selection. Open daily in summer, Wednesday through Sunday in winter (PO Box 160, Neah Bay; 360/645-2711).

***Neah Bay Tour.*** For an in-depth look at this whole area, sign up for a Native American Adventure. Donna Wilkie (PO Box 57, Neah Bay; 360/645-2554 or 360/645-2201) will tailor a tour to suit your schedule. The one-hour tour covers the museum. The two-hour tour adds a circle of the town and the five historic villages that it encompasses, plus a trip up to a vantage point from which you can photograph Tatoosh Island. In three hours, she'll show you all of the above, plus the ocean beaches and nearby archaeological sites.

# OLYMPIC NATIONAL PARK

What draws most visitors to the Olympic Peninsula is Olympic National Park, a massive expanse that offers both mountains and seashore. There's something fascinating and a little mysterious about this 922,000-acre wilderness, with its almost impenetrable core of snow-clad peaks; its deep river valleys radiating out to sea, strait, or sound; and its miles of primitive ocean beaches.

The main body of the park occupies the heart of the peninsula, encompassing the rugged peaks, dense rain forests, and wild river valleys of the Olympic Mountains. Along the Pacific Coast stretch another 57 miles of park, with forested headlands, isolated beaches, spectacular sea stacks, and pounding surf.

Highway 101 makes a great loop around the peninsula, tracing the northern border of the park, then turning south to run between the mountains and the ocean and continuing eastward and northward to parallel the eastern edge of the park.

The ideal way to experience the park is slowly. Take time to seek out meadows aglow with wildflowers, spooky rain forests, rivers to raft or paddle, beaches to comb, trails to hike, country stores to browse, and small-town life to savor. The visitor who has only a few days would do well to concentrate on one area instead of doing the entire loop. If you have a week, drive a few hours, then stop to find lodging or camping and see what the area has to offer. The towns along the park's perimeter offer meals from hot dogs to haute cuisine, and lodgings from hostels to some of the state's most highly regarded bed-and-breakfast inns. When you get into town, head for the tourist information center where people are eager to help you and offer reliable advice. For a traditional national park experience, stop at one of the five history-steeped lodges: Lake Crescent Lodge, Log Cabin Resort, Sol Duc Hot Springs Resort, Kalaloch Lodge, and Lake Quinault Lodge. The two main Olympic National Park visitor centers are in Port Angeles and at the end of the Hoh River Road, south of Forks.

***Roosevelt elk are named for Teddy Roosevelt—who first set aside a preserve that eventually became Olympic National Park—not for FDR, who actually created the park. To be sure of seeing an elk while on the peninsula, stop at the visitor center on the way to Hurricane Ridge, where a handsome Roosevelt elk stands tall in the Olympic Forest exhibit.***

## HURRICANE RIDGE TO THE ELWHA RIVER

From Port Angeles and other points along the Strait of Juan de Fuca, the Olympic Mountains tower on the southern horizon like an icy, impenetrable fortress, defending the alpine wonderland at the heart of the park. No roads traverse the mountainous core. In the surrounding national forests, however, rough logging roads snake over slopes and crisscross valleys, providing access to 600 miles of wilderness trails. From then on it's footpower or, on some trails, horsepower. Most of the ocean strip between Cape Alava and Kalaloch is also inaccessible by road. Yet within a half-hour drive from Highway 101, you can stand atop a high alpine ridge, soak in a hot spring, canoe a lake, hike a forest trail, wander a deep river valley, or raft a river.

### ACTIVITIES

***Visitor Center.*** Most people access the mountainous section of Olympic National Park from Port Angeles, site of the main visitor center. From Highway 101 east of town drive south on Race Road for about 2 miles to the Olympic National Park Visitors Center (3002 Mount Angeles Road; 360/452-0330). Knowledgeable staff will help you plan your outing, whether a backpack hike through the park (perhaps following the historic and rugged route of the Press Expedition in 1890) or a day trip to Hurricane Ridge. The grounds around the center are planted with native shrubs and plants, helpfully identified with signs. It's an open, inviting space, where the kids may be allowed to run and play. Young and old can let off still more steam by hiking the undemanding Peabody Creek Trail, to the west of the parking lot, a mile-long loop through the woods down to the burbling creek and back.

***Hurricane Ridge.*** From the Olympic National Park Visitors Center south of Port Angeles, follow Heart o' the Hills Parkway for 17 winding, scenic miles to the lodge, trails, and spectacular views of Hurricane Ridge. From the mile-high summit, you can see north to Canada and south to the inner Olympics, where the monarch of them all, 7,965-foot Mount Olympus, is enthroned. The terrace below the lodge on the south has helpful displays of the whole range, so you can learn which mountain is which. The lodge, open from Memorial Day to mid-September and during the ski season, offers ranger talks, snacks, ski rentals, a gift shop, and naturalist-guided snowshoe walks on winter weekends (snowshoes provided free). Paved trails run up gentle slopes from the parking area through fields of wildflowers in summer—or patchy snow in fall and spring—to the ridge, with its subalpine firs wind-sculpted into bonsai shapes. At the end of Hurricane Ridge Road, a popular nature trail leads to 5,757-foot Hurricane Hill (3 miles round-trip) with its 360-degree view. Hint to wildflower watchers: Come in June or July and treat yourself to one of the most beautiful—and accessible—displays in the whole park. Wheelchairs can navigate the first half-mile of the trail. Picnic areas are frequent along the road to Hurricane Hill; so are gray jays, which will shamelessly beg for a bite of your sandwich. Hurricane Ridge is the peninsula's only downhill ski area, with two rope tows and one poma lift. It's popular with cross-country skiers but it can be chancy, with icy conditions. The road is usually open weekends in winter; call 360/452-0329 to get the latest info.

***On the way up to Hurricane Ridge, and all around the lodge at the summit, you're almost sure to see deer who may tell you they are hungry. Pay no attention. It's against park regulations to feed the animals. But they generally make compliant models for photos.***

***For current weather and road conditions at Hurricane Ridge, and visibility from the ridge, call 360/452-0329.***

***High Drive.*** Six miles east of Port Angeles turn south from Highway 101 on Deer Park Road, a 17-mile, one-lane unpaved road (summer only) that winds up to Deer Park, where you'll find alpine meadows, picnic and camping sites, and vast views. Endemic plants, such as the shy Flett's violet, attract native-plant enthusiasts. Listen for the whistle of the marmots and watch browsing deer. An old fire road takes you to the highest point you can reach by road in the park, 6,000-foot Blue Mountain, where you may find yourself above the clouds, immersed in swirling fog, or with an unobstructed 360-degree view.

***High-Ridge Hike.*** Between Deer Park and the trailhead at Obstruction Peak (8 miles by narrow gravel road from Hurricane Ridge), a 7½-mile trail follows the ridgeline. Once the idea was to build a road between the two points, but impassable obstructions at Obstruction Peak put an end to that, to the joy of present-day hikers. You'll feel as if you're on top of the world. Make it a day hike if you can leave a car at one end; or hike west to east, camp at Deer Park, and retrace your steps next day. It's windy up there—bring your kite.

***The Elwha is one of the park's more placid rivers, and there's no age or experience limit for rafters with Olympic Raft and Kayak Service. "I've guided more than a thousand trips down the Elwha," says owner David King, "and ages have run from 5 to 95."***

***Raft the Elwha.*** From April to early September, Olympic Raft and Guide Service (239521 Highway 101, 12 miles west of Port Angeles where the Elwha River Road meets Highway 101; 360/452-1443) offers raft trips on the Elwha (from Altair Campground to the Elwha Store on 101) and the Hoh (from near Minnie Peterson Ranch to Oxbow Canyon). Even tyro rafters take to it right away, wielding their oars enthusiastically and squealing at the white-water bumpy spots—which are not really threatening. Owner-guide David King, who is licensed by Olympic National Park, points out mergansers, harlequin ducks, deer, and kingfishers along the way. He also offers half-day kayaking trips at Freshwater Bay on the strait, on Lake Aldwell, and on the Hoh.

## LAKE CRESCENT

In Pleistocene times, a 3,000-foot-thick glacier sculpted Lake Crescent, at the same time carving out the Strait of Juan de Fuca, Hood Canal, and Puget Sound. The very deep, very blue lake, 20 miles west of Port Angeles, is still relatively pristine, since it is surrounded by national park land and protected from development. Highway 101 hugs its south shore, with many pullouts for picnicking and leg stretching.

***Lake Crescent is home to Kamloops and Crescenti trout, as well as the legendary Beardslee, the landlocked trout that lurks in the lake's depths and nowhere else. To see a plump, silver-blue stuffed example, visit the lobby of Log Cabin Resort.***

## ACTIVITIES

***A Pair of Year-Round Hikes.*** Unlike the Olympic Park high country, Lake Crescent is hospitable to hikers even in winter. For the Marymere Falls hike, get directions at the Storm King Ranger Station at Barnes Point. Here one of the park's loveliest little walks begins. It's a 2-mile, round-trip stroll along a bouncy trail carpeted with forest duff (steep only at the approach to the falls, and wheelchair-accessible to that point), in the shade of giant firs, cedars, and maples. The 90-foot falls springing out of the ferny cliff are your reward, visible (but a challenge to photographers) from a viewing platform at trail's end. On the other side of the lake, the 4-mile Spruce Railroad Trail follows the route of a short-lived railroad built during World War I to get spruce timber, needed for airplanes, out of the woods. The war ended before the first load was shipped but the roadbed makes a wonderfully flat and pleasant trail. From the west, follow Camp David Road 4.7 miles from Fairholm to the trailhead at its end; from the east, follow East Beach Road 4 miles from Highway 101 to a trailhead near Log Cabin Resort. You'll see remains of a closed railroad tunnel and the deep Devil's Punch Bowl, spanned by a high, arched footbridge. Looking down into the translucent depths, a hiker on the bridge may see fish swimming 50 feet below.

***Last-Chance Store.*** Fairholm General Store & Cafe, at the west end of Lake Crescent (221121 Highway 101; 360/928-3020) is the last grocery for the westbound traveler for 17 miles. Homemade soups and baked goods, camping supplies, and guidebooks are available, as well as rental canoes and rowboats for use on Lake Crescent.

***Wilderness Classrooms.*** Olympic Park Institute (111 Barnes Point Road, north of Highway 101; 360/928-3720; opi@yni.org; www.yni.org/opi), is headquartered within the park at Rosemary Lodge on the lake shore just east of Lake Crescent Lodge. OPI dispenses knowledge, fun, fresh air, and companionship through its field seminars, some daylong, most weekend-long. Some include lodging and meals; others, which range to distant shores or into the mountains, require camping. Sleeping accommodations are in dorm-type cabins with bunk beds. Meals are hearty and unfailingly tasty, prepared by health-conscious cooks, and are served buffet-style in the rustic lodge. This historic building was a famous resort in the 1920s; the fireplace room is now a lounge-lecture hall, and upstairs bedrooms are labs and classrooms with microscopes and slide projectors. Instructors are first-rate, combining impressive knowledge with a talent for informal instruction. The current catalog lists five dozen courses relating to the Olympic outdoors, including birds, flowers, nature photography, Indian prehistory, tidepooling, ancient forests, and edible wild plants. Seminars run from mid-May to mid-October. Rosemary Lodge is also the site for a number of Elderhostel sessions. By planning an OPI session back-to-back with your own private explorations of the park and peninsula, you could come up with a really in-depth Olympic experience.

***"How I regret wasting 40 years of my life without knowing about nettle soup and lamb's lettuce salad."—Participant in ethnobotany seminar at Olympic Park Institute.***

***A Dip in the Pool.*** As if glaciated mountains, rain forests, and ocean beaches weren't enough, the Olympic Peninsula also has two accessible natural hot springs: Olympic, east of Lake

*According to the Indian legend, Sol Duc Hot Springs were formed when two lightning fish waged a battle in the Olympic Mountains, ending in a standoff. They were so anguished that they wept, and their tears gave birth to the hot springs.*

Crescent, and Sol Duc to the west. For the first and wilder of the two hot-springs experiences, drive the Elwha River Road south from Highway 101 and turn right on Boulder Creek Road at Lake Mills. (Pause here to look at the mossy old Glines Canyon Dam, which created serene Lake Mills but drowned one of the most spectacular and salmon-rich stretches of the Elwha.) Follow Boulder Creek Road to the end, and hike 2.4 miles to Olympic Hot Springs. The half-dozen rock-walled pools range from tepid to very hot. Once this was a posh resort; now it's back to nature and some visitors take that literally, applying themselves to the pools in the buff. (For directions to the Sol Duc springs, see the Lake Crescent to Sappho section of this chapter.)

## LODGINGS

### LAKE CRESCENT LODGE ★

View Built 80 years ago as Singer's Tavern, when guests came by boat, Lake Crescent Lodge is well worn but well maintained. The historic main building has a glassed-in veranda overlooking the lake, a lobby with a huge stone fireplace, an okay restaurant, and a very hospitable bar. The upstairs rooms are noisy and rustic—a euphemism that means, among other things, that the bathroom is down the hall. The motel rooms are the best for the money, but the tiny cabins, all in a row overlooking the lake, with porches and fireplaces, can be fun (if you bear in mind that they were built in 1937, back when President Franklin Roosevelt came to visit just before he created Olympic National Park). The service is just fine—mainly enthusiastic college kids having a nice summer. *416 Lake Crescent Rd, Port Angeles; 20 miles west of Port Angeles on Hwy 101; 360/928-3211; $$; AE, DC, MC, V; checks OK; closed Nov to May.*

### LOG CABIN RESORT

View Located on the "sunny side of Lake Crescent," this old-time resort has served visitors for over a century, although none of the present buildings are over 70 years old, and some are a great deal younger. The wide variety of accommodations offer few frills, but are very livable. Lakeside chalets sleep six when using the upstairs loft, and although there is a refrigerator, cooking must be done outside on a barbecue. Some cabins have full kitchenettes. Campers happily make do with the one-room log cabins with electricity but no indoor plumbing. The restaurant is adequate, and the sheltered patio is a pleasant dining spot. *3183 East Beach Rd, Port Angeles; 15 miles west of Port Angeles and 3 miles north of Hwy 101 on East Beach Rd; 360/928-3325; $$; DC, MC, V; checks OK; closed Oct to May.*

## LAKE CRESCENT TO SAPPHO

Follow a long, westward reach of Highway 101, which forges its way through second-growth forest and provides access to hiking trails and campgrounds. At tiny Sappho (gas, grocery, bus stop), Highway 101 meets Highway 113, which takes off to the north to Highway 112 and the northwest corner of the peninsula.

## ACTIVITIES

***Sol Duc Hot Springs.*** Watch for Soleduck Road, which turns south from Highway 101 about 3 miles west of Lake Crescent, and drive 12 miles up through impressive old-growth forest to Sol Duc Resort, where the hot springs are part of the attraction and the nearby trailheads for some of the park's most glorious hikes are the rest. Whether you arrive by car or by foot after days of hiking snow-bordered mountain trails, these hot springs are the ideal trail's end. The Quileute Indians called the area "Sol Duc"—a land of sparkling water. In the early 1900s, a grand hotel here was a mecca for affluent travelers seeking relief from their aches and pains. Now Sol Duc Hot Springs Resort occupies the grounds. You need not be a guest at the resort to take your dip. For about $6, you can have a hot soak, followed by a swim in a cold pool; you can also opt for a lengthy massage. Open daily mid-May to end of September; weekends only, October and April to mid-May; closed November through March; 360/327-3583.

***High-Country Hikes.*** An easy hike from the resort (1.5 miles round-trip) to nearby Soleduck Falls passes through a magnificent stand of old-growth forest, leading to a footbridge from which even an all-thumbs photographer can snap a great picture of one of the most-photographed waterfalls in the park.

The Soleduck campground is favored by backpackers taking off for the high country, including popular Seven Lakes Basin, a four-star wilderness hike to a valley full of jewellike tarns. Permits to camp here are now necessary; call 360/452-0330 or get advice at the Soleduck Ranger Station.

***Take Fido for a Walk.*** Mount Muller Trail is in National Forest and Department of Natural Resources land, so dogs may accompany the hiker. The trailhead is half a mile off Highway 101, about 4¾ miles west of Fairholm at milepost 216. The trail runs 13 miles to 3,748-foot Mount Muller, with sensational views of Mount Baker, the Strait of Juan de Fuca, Mount Olympus, and Lake Crescent. You'll go past alpine meadows, brimming with wildflowers in July and August, and the huge boulder formation known as Fout's Rock House.

## LODGINGS

### SOL DUC HOT SPRINGS RESORT

Surrounded by forest, 32 small, cedar-roofed sleeping cabins are clustered in the grassy meadow. The favorites are those with porches facing the river. Up to four adults and two kids can share a cabin, though it'll be a pretty cozy fit. The duplex units have kitchens, and in keeping with the natural serenity there are no TVs anywhere and a no-smoking policy everywhere. Camping and RV sites are available. The Springs Restaurant is open for breakfast and dinner; a snack deli near the pool is open midday. Hot springs and pool use are included in the cabin rental fee. The resort is open May through September; open weekends only, October and April; and closed from November through March. *PO Box 2169, Port Angeles; 12 miles south of Hwy 101, west of Lake Crescent; 360/327-3583; $$; AE, MC, V; checks OK.*

# LAKE OZETTE AND OCEAN BEACHES

The 50-mile stretch of the Pacific Coast from Lake Ozette to Queets—much of it within the coastal strip of Olympic National Park—is about as wild as it gets, with awesome beaches, both sandy and rockbound, and windswept spruces crowding along the cliffs. This is timber country; on its way to the coast, Highway 101 threads its way through clearcuts, flourishing replanted forests, and mature giants, with here and there a valley affording a view of bucolic farms and, rarely, a glimpse of the Olympic Mountains. South of Forks, Highway 101 skirts the famed rain forests of Olympic National Park, with three spur roads poking eastward into the park, up the Hoh, Queets, and Quinault Rivers. All lead to trailheads for further exploration of the Olympics. After crossing the Hoh, Highway 101 returns to the coast and your reward is access to some sensational beaches. As you approach Kalaloch, well-marked trails from Highway 101 point the way. This is a different face of Olympic National Park: the mountains are invisible, the wilderness seashore and the coastal rain forest dominate the landscape. Even when fog dims the view, the sound of the surf and the wind on your face, laden with moisture, tell you that this is the wild and westernmost edge of the continent. Services are few and far between along this stretch, so plan ahead.

***"I'm too busy to get lonesome," said Lars Ahlstrom, when asked how he stood living alone on his prairie. "If I do, I put a good polka on the phonograph and dance a whirl with myself."***

The northernmost access to the ocean strip of Olympic National Park is from Lake Ozette, the state's largest natural lake. Although the lake is directly west of Highway 101, you must take the northern route—Highway 112 from Port Angeles—to reach it. One mile west of Sekiu turn south; then follow the 20-mile Hoko-Ozette Road to its end. Camping and picnicking by the lake are permitted year-round. Ozette is a grand canoeing lake, but take care—winds can whip up in a hurry.

## ACTIVITIES

***The Lake Ozette Loop.*** From Lake Ozette, you may hike a triangular 9-mile course to the ocean, down along the shore and back by Sand Point Trail; or choose just the first leg, a nonstrenuous 6-mile round-trip walk to Cape Alava, much of it on a puncheon trail (cedar slabs). En route you come out of the woods onto Ahlstrom's Prairie, a broad, sunlit clearing where elk sometimes browse. A few fragmentary timbers bear witness to homesteader Lars Ahlstrom's residence here from 1902 to 1958. At the beach, there's little evidence of the energetic archaeological dig here that uncovered a 500-year-old, mud-buried Makah village in the early '70s. A cedar hut and a plaque summarize the story; the artifacts unearthed are brilliantly displayed at the Makah Museum at Neah Bay. From Cape Alava, you can retrace your steps to Lake Ozette, or head south along the beach to Sand Point (3 miles), watching for the Indian petroglyphs at Wedding Rocks along the way, then hike back to Ozette through the woods. Or you may camp on the beach. Permits are required; they're free but issued in limited numbers. Call 360/452-0300.

***The Marine Sanctuary.*** The new Pacific Coast National Marine Sanctuary stretches from Cape Flattery south to Copalis. It runs seaward 30 to 40 miles, encompassing 3,300 square miles, within which are 870 offshore islands. The sanctuary is managed by the National Oceanic and Atmospheric Administration (NOAA) (local offices at 138 W 1st Street, Port Angeles; 360/457-6622), and was established in 1994 to protect marine resources and to maintain the coast's natural and cultural heritage. As you roam these beaches, you are still welcome to fish, hike, camp, and gather shellfish; that's the whole idea—to preserve the area for responsible recreational use. The prohibited activities are exploration for oil and gas, removal of historical or cultural resources, injuring or harvesting marine mammals, and low-flying aircraft.

## FORKS

This little town is the unofficial capital of what is known as the West End of the Olympic Peninsula. The timber heritage is still proudly remembered, but with the decline of logging, tourism is taking over, without the crowds. From Forks you can explore sparsely peopled coastal beaches; take a chance at hooking a steelhead; go mountain biking, camping, fishing, or hiking; climb Mt. Olympus; or hunker down in a wilderness lodge. Bed-and-breakfasts have popped up to suit every taste—with rates still quite reasonable by east-of-the-Sound standards.

The Chamber of Commerce's Visitor Information Center at the south edge of town, next to the Timber Museum, has tips on what to do, where to stay, and more, cheerfully dispensed (along with free coffee) by Director Diane Schostak and her volunteers. For advance help, e-mail them (chamber@olypen.com) or consult the web site (www.forkswa.com). Or call 360/374-2531 or 800/44-FORKS.

## ACTIVITIES

***Drop in at the Raindrop.*** At this modest cafe at 111 S Forks Avenue (Highway 101; 360/374-6612) Mary Springer, who has been winning cooking prizes practically since she was a toddler, serves up a mean burger, though not as mean as the names imply (the Rolling Thunder Burger and Lightning Bolt, to name a couple), and disgracefully rich chocolate cakes. The fountain choices include good old-fashioned banana splits and root-beer floats. Stop in for breakfast, lunch, or dinner.

***"Visitors are surprised that we have so many creative people out here," says Susan Shaw, Forks mixed-media artist. "I think one reason is all the rain. When we can't get out, we have to find some outlet for our energy. When it rains, I just go into my studio and get to work, and I'm perfectly happy."***

***Timber!*** On the southern outskirts of Forks, the Timber Museum—a sturdy structure built by volunteer labor, including the local high school carpentry class—tells the story of the West End's logging heritage. Stop where you see the two chainsaw-carved, rugged timber workers sawing away at a huge log. Another nearby carving of a 16-foot-tall logger is a tribute to those who have lost their lives in the woods. 1421 S Forks Avenue (Highway 101); 360/374-9663.

***Art on the Go.*** Ask at the Visitor Center about Arttrek, a self-guided tour of nearly two dozen studios, galleries, and gift shops from La Push to Lake Crescent, from Kalaloch to Neah Bay, and all over Forks. You'll be given a free map and list of painters, spinners, purveyors of handcrafts and antiques, and more. Each displays a big Arttrek sign when open so visitors know they're welcome. Participant Dennis Chastain of Den's Wood Den (181433 Highway 101, Forks; 360/374-5079), carved the giant logger at the Timber Museum.

***Take a Tour—or Two.*** During the summer you may hop on a logging crew bus for a Logging and Mill Tour: visit a working lumber mill, inspect the world's largest red cedar, and see how old bridge beams are recycled into flooring. Or join a wild-plant expert for a woodland walk, and learn how Native Americans found uses for skunk cabbage and horsetail. Tours are free; get schedules and make reservations at the Visitor Information Center or call 360/374-2531.

***A Trail Less Traveled.*** The Bogachiel River Trail, at the end of Undi Road, which goes east from Highway 101 at Bogachiel State Park, a few miles south of Forks, is a rain-forest hike almost as good as the Hoh but with far fewer people. Six miles in is Bogachiel Shelter, a reasonable destination for weekend hikers. The trail, leading through lush forests, is mostly flat and follows the river but can be mushy and slushy in the rain. But you knew you were coming to the rain forest, so of course you packed your waterproof gear.

***Shortest rain forest hike is an almost half-mile loop trail behind the Forks Timber Museum, which combines nature study with fitness: trees and shrubs are identified, and a variety of exercise and muscle-building aids are located along the trail. Watch out for joggers and power walkers—or become one. To get more of a workout, walk on up the hill on a new trail that leads to the handsome new Olympic Natural Resources Center, go in and learn about forests and fish, and see works of local artists on display.***

## RESTAURANTS

### SMOKE HOUSE RESTAURANT

Stop at the big blue building north of Forks for a sampling of what the food in these parts is all about. The salmon is alder-smoked on the premises and this moist, lightly smoked fish is the star ingredient on the restaurant's menu. Try it as an entree, in sandwiches, tossed with pasta, or in a salad. Some have found the service erratic, especially on busy weekend evenings, but in general the waitresses know most everyone, go out of their way to make strangers welcome, and gladly dispense travel advice. Take home a tasty souvenir—the restaurant sells cans of its private-label salmon. *193161 Hwy 101, Forks; north of town at the junction of Hwy 101 and La Push Rd; 360/374-6258; $; MC, V; checks OK; lunch, dinner every day; full bar.*

## LODGINGS

### BEAR CREEK HOMESTEAD ★

View

At the end of the road, in a meadowy little valley homesteaded by sturdy Norwegian immigrants, this bed-and-breakfast is the kind of place where you'd like to move right in and let Sherry and Larry Baysinger adopt you. It isn't grand: a 75-year-old house, which the Baysingers remodeled to offer two rooms with private baths and a hospitable living room, and an open farm kitchen. Besides the usual homey amenities—patchwork quilts, fresh flowers (maybe a vase of the original homesteaders' roses), and rocking chairs—you'll appreciate the thoughtful little touches. At the tea station in the hall near the bedrooms, you'll find yourself gathering as though at the water cooler to chat with fellow guests while brewing your cup of chamomile or cocoa. Take it into your room and there's a home-baked cinnamon roll on your bedside table. If you come back damp from a hike or a fishing trip, head for the woodstove and boot dryers in the barn, then for the hot tub under the stars. The place is TV-free but there are plenty of books and the player piano makes beautiful music. Kids have a ball making friends with the llamas, the goats, and a couple of comical grandstanding dogs. Down at the end of the field Bear Creek murmurs on its way to the Soleduck; here you just might reel in a rainbow trout or steelhead. The Baysingers are putting a couple of outfitters' tents down by the creek for folks who want to camp but might like to walk up to the inn for a country breakfast. Sherry's meals are bounteous and feature eggs fresh from the nest and fruit just plucked from the tree or vine. *209 Bear Creek Rd; west on Bear Creek Rd at milepost 206, Hwy 101, 15 miles north of Forks; 360/327-3699; www.northolympic.com/bch; baysngr@olypen.com; $$; MC, V; checks OK.*

***For Olympic adventures, put yourself in the hands of Sol Duc Valley Packers, an enterprise of Larry and Sherry Baysinger, who run Bear Creek Homestead. They'll provide guide referral or a back-country hike without backache: Larry and his crew pack in everything and set up camp for you. They'll even carry your gear to base camp so you can scale Mount Olympus or the mountain of your choice; 360/327-3699.***

## BRIGHTWATER HOUSE ★

There's no sign on Highway 101, no brochure in the tourist center, and it's at the end of an obscure lane off one of the maze of roads that lead from Forks to La Push and the ocean beaches. How do people find this lodge hidden away in the lower Soleduck rain forest? For serious fly fishermen—which about a third of the guests are—it's probably instinct. For the rest it's largely word-of-mouth. The rambling inn is surrounded by lawns, vigorous rhododendrons, barns, and a still-productive 80-year-old orchard. Richard Chesnore, who with his wife Beth runs the inn, says he doesn't have to worry about harvesting the apples and pears: "The elk come through and vacuum the lot." Chesnore, an archaeologist, has discovered the outhouse and many artifacts of the original homesteaders. Hospitality is up to the minute. The master bedroom has a private deck and patio and a river view. Upstairs there's a spacious two-room fireplace suite. When you retire in this comfortable retreat it's easy to forget you're in the Olympic wilderness—until you hear the yipping of the coyotes. The breakfast table offers a prime

***The Forks Old-Fashioned Fourth of July Celebration is a blast, with a salmon barbecue, games for young and old, fireworks, and a parade that stars the best-polished logging trucks in the West. Even the logs are scrubbed.***

view toward the river, and such enticements as quiches, a frittata with spinach and feta, and fresh fruits. But no Soleduck steelhead; fishing here is strictly catch-and-release, which is the way Chesnore and the dedicated sportsmen who cast their lines from the inn's 3,500 feet of river frontage want it. *440 Brightwater Dr, PO Box 1222, Forks; left at first intersection on Hwy 110, left on Brightwater Dr; 360/374-5453; www.northolympic.com/; $$; MC, V; checks OK.*

### EAGLE POINT INN ★★

Cradled on 5 acres in a bend of the Soleduck River, this spacious log lodge was especially designed by Chris and Dan Christensen to blend comfort and style in a matchless wilderness setting. The two downstairs bedrooms, each with queen-size beds covered with thick down comforters, have spacious bathrooms. The open two-story common living quarters house Chris's collection of kerosene lamps and other interesting antiques, leaving enough room to spread out, perhaps to relax in front of the fireplace made of rocks from the river. Even if you need to get up before dawn to fish, a hearty breakfast will be ready when you are (and ever-attentive Chris also fixes picnic lunches on request). A covered outdoor kitchen down near the river is ideal for barbecuing your own meal at night. *384 Stormin' Norman Lane, PO Box 546, Beaver WA 98305; between Forks and Sappho on Hwy 101; go east on Stormin' Norman Lane at milepost 202; 360/327-3236; $$; no credit cards; checks OK.*

### HUCKLEBERRY LODGE ★

This Forks bed-and-breakfast has carved out a niche as a choice destination for fishers, hunters, and gatherers (lots of mushrooms and huckleberries in those woods). Kitty and Bill Sperry offer fishing and hunting packages plus sound advice if you want to go on your own. Bring your ideas and your hosts will help make them happen: llama trekking, an ATV trail ride, walking on the wild ocean beaches, mountain biking. After a day of play come back to wind down, maybe with a game of pool in the family room and a soak in the hot tub and sauna. Less ambitious folks hang around the inn, perhaps to walk through the woods to the riverside, then snuggle down in the living room by the fire under the benign gaze of the mounted heads on the wall: elk, moose, and a black bison. A stroll through the inn is like a visit to a Native American museum plunked down in Hemingway country. The Sperrys have a fine collection of Native art, including masks, baskets, beadwork, and deerskin dance dresses, as well as the hunting trophies. You'll find a variety of accommodation choices. Besides three rooms in the inn (one very elegant, with antiques, a beautifully draped headboard for the king bed, and mirrored doors on the huge closet), there are a few RV hookup spots, and four cabin units. One is like a little apartment with sitting room, bedroom, and kitchen; of the others, our favorite has two queen beds with bright patchwork quilts, a kitchenette, and a little loft inhabited by a stuffed cougar. *1171 Big Pine Way, Forks; east of Hwy 101, just north of town; 888/822-6008 or 360/374-6008; $$–$$$; MC, V; checks OK.*

***For a preview of Elizabeth Barlow's works, evocative of country life, and of others on the Art-trek route, visit the West Wind Gallery in Forks (71 N Forks Avenue; 360/374-7795), which shares quarters with Espresso Elegante and a bookstore and antique gallery.***

## MANITOU LODGE ☆

View

Once it was a private hunting and fishing lodge and that flavor persists, what with the shingled exterior and the 2½-story Great Room with its huge fieldstone fireplace. It's easy to imagine the host and his guests lolling in their chairs, sipping their brandies and comparing notes on the ones that did or didn't get away. Fishing still brings people, many for the winter steelhead run—the Bogachiel joins the Soleduck just a couple of stone's throws from the Manitou's driveway. Other attractions: ocean beaches (it's only 4 miles to Rialto Beach) and easy drives to the Hoh rain forest, Lake Ozette, and Cape Flattery. Stay-at-home types are content to head out on nearby trails to look for eagles and hummingbirds, mushrooms, or elk, and to hang out in the Great Room or swing in the hammock under the towering evergreens. Innkeepers Ed and Lynne Murphy are knowledgeable about Northwest Native American art and it sets the tone for the inn decor. They offer baskets, beadwork, and jewelry in a small gift shop. The six rooms in the lodge include the choice Sacajawea Suite with its marble fireplace and king bed; all have their own outside entrances. In the two-unit cottage, Eagle has a mini kitchenette; and in Owl the window frames a picture that captures the essence of the rain forest—a huge spruce, moss-hung branches, and huckleberry bushes with their red berries gleaming in the shadows. Breakfast is on a large scale: hearty offerings of eggs Benedict, waffles, and the works, served with a forest view. *Kilmer Rd, PO Box 600, Forks; 8 miles west of Hwy 101 on Hwy 110, right on Mora Rd, right on Kilmer Rd; 360/374-6295; manitou@olypen.com; www.manitoulodge.com; $$; AE, DC, MC, V; checks OK.*

### MILLER TREE INN ★

View It's the granddaddy of Forks bed-and-breakfasts, set back from the road in a cluster of large firs, spruces, cedars, and an uncommonly tall monkey-puzzle tree. Just a few blocks east of Highway 101, the inn is surrounded by the pastures of the original homestead, where it's not unusual to see herds of elk grazing. It's now run by Bill and Susan Brager, who have preserved the relaxed atmosphere while adding amenities. Of the seven rooms, three have private baths, the others have half-baths or share. The living room is a comfortable spot to relax or play a game of Monopoly, lemonade is served on the lawn in summer, and the kitchen is not off limits if you just ask. Fisherfolk appreciate the predawn breakfasts, their hosts' knowledge of local river conditions, the facilities for cleaning and freezing the catch, and the hot tub to relax in after a day on the river. Breakfasts may offer gingerbread pancakes with lemon sauce or blueberry French toast, and choices from the breakfast bar—cereal, fruit and pastries. Children over 7 and well-mannered pets are welcome. *654 E Division St, Forks; 6th St and E Division, next to City Hall; 360/374-6806; MC, V; $; checks OK.*

## LA PUSH

***Beaches near La Push use ordinal numbers (e.g., First Beach) and those between Ruby Beach and Kalaloch use cardinal numbers (e.g., Beach 6).***

The Dickey, Calawah, Bogachiel, and Soleduck Rivers all merge and enter the ocean as the Quillayute River near La Push, a little seaside community 17 miles west of Forks. La Push, center of the ancestral lands of the Quileutes, has a 96-slip marina where the local fleet shelters and where sports fishermen may launch their skiffs. Offshore is fortress-like James Island, site of an ancient Quileute village. To the north and south of La Push extend miles of wilderness coastline, much of it within the ocean strip of Olympic National Park. It's the last such stretch remaining in the United States outside of Alaska. The lure of the Pacific wilderness coast, with its jagged offshore sea stacks and teeming tidepools, brings venturesome beach hikers. Rolling combers bring surfers and fearless sea kayakers.

## ACTIVITIES

***Where the Rivers Meet.*** Three Rivers Resort (7764 La Push Road; junction of La Push and Mora Roads; 360/374-5300) is almost within casting distance of the confluence of the Bogachiel, Soleduck, and Quillayute Rivers, where salmon and steelhead leap. The resort offers guided fishing trips and can put you in touch with guides for backpacking on the beach, llama pack trips in the park, and rain-forest field trips. The store has basic necessities, and in the cafe you may choose between two hearty River Burgers: the Bogie and the Quil. Also find soups, sandwiches, 12 flavors of shakes and malts, and espresso. The five housekeeping cabins are modest at best; there are also RV hookups and campsites. La Push and ocean beaches are only five minutes away.

***Cabins by the Sea.*** The only lodging in La Push is Ocean Park/Shoreline Resorts, a Quileute tribal enterprise; 800/487-1267 or 360/374-5267. The resort is not what it once was, but it still commands outstanding views of the ocean, and offers a variety of accommodations from motel-style units to primitive cabins. Best bet: the newer, fireplace cabins with kitchens and unobstructed ocean views.

***Wild Ocean Beaches.*** La Push is access point to a bevy of unfrequented beaches. Farthest north is Rialto (take Mora Road to the right from the La Push Road, a couple of miles before you get to town). Rialto Beach offers picnicking, smelting in season, and ranger-guided naturalist walks from nearby Mora campground, and is the jump-off spot for a three-day wilderness beach hike north to Cape Alava and Lake Ozette. Three beaches south of La Push are easy to approach for a day excursion: broad, sandy First Beach is just beyond the driftwood and jetty south of town; signs on the La Push road point to trails to Second and Third

***All ocean beaches can be extremely dangerous due to fluctuating tides and unfordable creeks during periods of heavy rain. Many headlands and sea stacks can't be skirted at high tide. If you plan an overnight hike from La Push, be sure to stop in at the ranger station in Mora to get a use permit and tide tables; 360/374-5460. "I don't know how many times a year we have to go rescue someone from a cliff," says a park ranger.***

Beaches. At Second Beach, see a dramatic sea stack near the shore, and peer into tidepools. Third Beach, separated from Second by impassable Teahwhit Head, also has tidepools, plus a waterfall near the south end. From here, begin the strenuous 16-mile hike south to the Hoh River, which requires several climbs over rugged heads that cannot be skirted on the shore.

## HOH RAIN FOREST

Easily accessible by the Upper Hoh Road, off Highway 101, 12 miles south of Forks, the Hoh Rain Forest is one of the wettest locations in the contiguous United States, with an average yearly rainfall of 142 inches. This steady moisture nurtures dense vegetation, with more than 3,000 species of plant life—including a giant Sitka spruce over 500 years old. After 19 miles the road ends at the Hoh River Visitor Center, the second major entry point to Olympic National Park (after the Port Angeles center).

## ACTIVITIES

***It's probably true that pioneer settler John Huelsdonk ("Iron Man of the Hoh") carried an iron cookstove on his back up the Hoh River trail to his homestead, back in the 1890s. But the end of the story is apocryphal: his only complaint was that the 50-pound sack of flour inside the stove kept shifting and made it hard to keep his balance.***

SHOPS ***Adventureland.*** Five miles up the Hoh River road, Peak 6 Adventure Store (4883 Upper Hoh Road, Forks; 360/374-5254) can help you prepare for hiking, climbing, or camping. Named for a peak in the Willoughby Range that looms behind the store, it's like a miniature REI close to where the goods will do the most good. Gary and Charlotte Peterson run it; he's the grandson of legendary Minnie Peterson, who led pack trips into the Olympics for 50 years. "About 200,000 people come up this road every summer," says Gary, "and a lot of them are heading for the mountains, maybe an Olympus climb. We're here to supply them with whatever they need, whether it's tent pegs or rainboots or a zero-degree sleeping bag." Peak 6 also caters to dawdlers, with an ice cream and espresso kiosk and umbrella tables.

***Last Chance for Hoh Burgers.*** A mile beyond Peak 6 is Mike Rasmusson's Hard Rain Cafe & Mercantile & RV Park (5763 Upper Hoh Road, Forks; 360/374-9288). Stop for a burger and a drink, relax at a picnic table on the deck or on the grass, or browse the store. You may find things you never dreamed you needed, from enamel washbasins to wild huckleberry gummi bears.

***Visitor Center.*** Though much of the approach from Highway 101 is through unprepossessing clearcuts, within the park the rain forest lives up to its promise, gloriously revealed at the visitor center, gateway to one of the unique ecosystems of the world. Good trails lead from the visitor center through groves of ancient, moss-laden giants: the Hall of Mosses Trail, an easy three-quarter-mile loop; and the Spruce Nature Trail, 1¼ miles round-trip. The latter and a short paved quarter-mile nature loop are wheelchair-accessible. You may see Roosevelt elk anywhere. The campground is open all year. If you get caught in the rain, dry off in the Interpretive Center while learning the difference between the Northwest's temperate rain forests (which are the world's largest) and the hot tropical ones.

***Hiking the Hoh.*** The Hoh River Trail, which continues upriver from the visitor center, is spectacular, winding through gigantic old-growth Sitka spruce, red cedar, bigleaf maple, and fir. It's ideal for families or beginning hikers because the first 13 miles or so are virtually flat, with fine campsites along the way. After that it gets steeper until you reach Glacier Meadows (17.5 miles), base camp for Mount Olympus climbing expeditions.

***The Lowdown on the Lower Hoh.*** About a mile south of the Upper Hoh Road, a turnoff to the west from Highway 101 points to the Hoh Indian Reservation. This is the Lower Hoh Road, also known as Oil City Road because of an unfulfilled 1930s dream of finding oil at the ocean's edge. The paved, then gravelly 11-mile road ends near the mouth of the Hoh and within earshot of the roar of Pacific breakers. Surf and river fishing and beachcombing lure some; for others, it's the start of the 16-mile beach hike north to La Push. For still others it's a pilgrimage to the studio of Elizabeth Barlow, multimedia artist and modest descendant of John Huelsdonk (Iron Man of the Hoh). Because her location is one of the more remote for artists on the Arttrek map, it's a good idea to call first before visiting; 360/374-6738.

## KALALOCH AREA

Highway 101 returns to the coast at Ruby Beach, your first taste of the line of accessible wilderness beaches that dot the coast for miles. Deceptively primitive now, Ruby Beach was once a flour-

***At Kalaloch, Olympic National Park staff lead daily beach and tidepool walks, and tours through coastal forests during the summer. Check at Kalaloch Lodge, or at the ranger station just down Highway 101.***

***Tidepools teem with fascinating creatures, but remember your tidepool etiquette: look, photograph, but don't disturb or remove the sealife.***

ishing resort, until the establishment of the ocean strip of Olympic National Park when all traces of civilization were erased. It offers rewarding beachcombing and a good view of Destruction Island to the southwest, and its own little Abbey Island, just offshore. Between Ruby Beach and Kalaloch Lodge, center of this coastal expanse, are Beaches 6, 4, 3, 2, and 1; the trail to Beach 5 has long been closed. Short, sometimes steep trails lead down to these beaches, each with its own appeal. Beach 4, one of the most spectacular, offers sheer rock walls, offshore sea stacks, and tidepools sheltering fascinating creatures. The upper parking lot has a wheelchair-accessible trail to a scenic overlook. Kalaloch Campground, just north of Kalaloch Lodge, is one of the park's most popular and its 175 sites fill up fast in the summer. Most of the beaches in the Kalaloch area are long and sandy, and tempt the beachcomber with sculptured driftwood, agates, jasper, and—very rarely nowadays—Japanese glass floats. Razor clamming is the thing in spring and fall, and smelting is big in summer. You can rent clam guns and smelt nets at the Kalaloch general store.

***Shellfish seekers in Washington State must have a license to go after oysters, crabs, and clams. Buy the license at any sporting goods or other store where fishing licenses are sold. For best value get the combo for $38.50: freshwater and salt water fishing plus shellfish.***

## ACTIVITIES

SHOPS ***Last Shopping Stop.*** Even if you don't stay at Kalaloch Lodge, be sure to stock up in its general store (157151 Highway 101; 360/962-2271). It's your last chance for quite a spell to lay in a supply of groceries, postcards, kites, paperbacks, and souvenirs. If you're southbound, the Kalaloch area is also your last opportunity for beach access for 50 miles.

## LODGINGS

### KALALOCH LODGE

This isolated lodge has become a habit for generations of beach buffs. The nearest town is 34 miles away, but the nearest beach is literally at your doorstep. The lodge perches above the mouth of Kalaloch Creek, looking out across the breaking surf to the wide Pacific. Accommodations include eight rooms and two suites in the lodge, most of which are refreshingly quiet, now that the upstairs bar has disappeared. Six have ocean views. Seacrest House, a modern, two-story lodging set amid wind-shaped trees, has some rooms with ocean-view decks. The four two-bedroom suites have wood-burning fireplaces and large living rooms; no kitchens, no ocean view, but plenty of seclusion. These are in great demand, especially during the holidays. Equally sought after are the newer log cabins with their small kitchen area (no utensils) and Franklin stove (complete with a stack of wood by the door). Couples favor the duplex cabins on the edge of the bluff. No phones or TVs. The restaurant's wide windows command a stupendous ocean view; staff are friendly if not always speedy, and the fare naturally leans toward tried-and-true seafood. The lounge has been abolished and now coexists with the coffee shop, and the reception desk is almost invisible in the crowded gift shop. A barbecue patio overlooks creek and sea, a place to grill your catch. Pets are allowed in cabins only. *157151 Hwy 101; 34 miles south of Forks; 360/962-2271; $$; AE, MC, V; checks OK.*

***The world's biggest Western Red Cedar—a 19-foot-diameter behemoth—is off Highway 101, 13.6 miles north of Kalaloch Lodge. Turn east on Nolan Creek Road (N1000), and follow the signs. (Get precise directions at the Kalaloch Ranger Station.)***

## QUEETS

Five miles south of Kalaloch is this tiny tribal village, part of the Quinault Indian Reservation. It's also near the west end of the Queets Corridor, a long skinny strip of Olympic National Park encompassing the Queets River, from mountains almost to sea. The Queets rain forest is practically deserted compared with the Hoh and is sought mostly by steelheaders and those who would camp or hike in solitude. Drive unpaved Queets River Road, which leaves Highway 101 7 miles east of Queets, for 10 miles through luxuriant forest to a small campground, a ranger station, and a trailhead for hiking farther up the river. You may see decaying remains of fences, barns, and cabins, as well as gnarled fruit trees and scattered garden flowers: until 1931 a colony of hardy homesteaders, called Evergreen on the Queets, lived here. A 3-mile loop trail from the campground meanders through old-growth and second-growth forest, and the overgrown fields of the pioneer homesteaders. Watch for elk grazing in grassy glades under moss-garlanded maples; and listen for their bugling.

***The Queets River campground is in a grove of giant spruce, some as much as 10 feet in diameter. Near the second entrance to the campground you can admire the biggest of all, 14 feet around at chest height.***

***Where's the biggest Sitka spruce in the state? You be the judge; both contenders are in Olympic National Park. One, plainly visible in the Queets campground, has the most volume, more than 10,000 cubic feet, and is taller (245 feet). Another, at the east end of Lake Quinault near Rain Forest Resort Village, has a greater circumference (59 feet) and crown spread.***

## LAKE QUINAULT

Lake Quinault's north shore marks the southern edge of Olympic National Park; its south shore is in the Olympic National Forest; and the lake itself is within the Quinault Indian Reservation. The quiet, glacier-carved lake reflects the dense evergreens that surround it, the fishing is memorable, and the tranquility is almost palpable. The few resorts around the lake are by and large respectful of their unique environment.

### ACTIVITIES

***Hikes and Walks.*** A number of easy lowland trails through old-growth forests are accessible from both the South and North Shore Roads. On the South Shore, the 3-mile Lake Quinault Loop starts near Lake Quinault Lodge, follows the lakeshore west, then enters Big Tree Grove—a stand of truly awesome 500-year-old Douglas firs. A shorter approach to Big Tree Grove is via the Rain Forest Nature Trail; look for the sign on South Shore Road near Willaby Campground. Uplake, the South Shore Road ends at Graves Creek Ranger Station, where day hikers may easily navigate the 1-mile Graves Creek Nature Trail. On the North Shore, drive 8.2 miles east from Highway 101 to the national park visitor center and explore the Maple Glade Rain Forest Interpretive Trail, a half-mile eye-opener to rain forest ecology and a favorite for hikers with children. Here, as well as at the ranger stations near Lake Quinault Lodge and at Graves Creek, you'll find information about these hikes, as well as on more strenuous hikes up the North Fork of the Quinault River or to Enchanted Valley, a 13-mile one-way journey up the East Fork. Experienced backpackers say this hike is as good as it gets in the park, maybe in the country. In the hidden-away alpine basin, waterfalls tumble down sheer cliffs on the north, the river meanders in braided courses through the valley, and a picturesque 1930s log chalet can accommodate hikers and horseback riders in emergencies. However, most people prefer to bed down in the meadow. A ranger is on duty during the summer. The Enchanted Valley trail keeps going right through the mountains and over Anderson Pass near Anderson Glacier, the most easily reached glacier in the park. The trail winds down the Dosewallips River, which flows into Hood Canal—end of a 30-mile cross-Olympic adventure.

***Less-traveled Trails.*** To get away from the crowds, consider alternative destinations that branch off the more popular trails. For example, one mile up the East Fork Quinault Trail, the Graves Creek Trail breaks south, leading about 8 miles up Graves Creek Canyon to Sundown Pass, and to Sundown Lake lying in its beautiful alpine basin, near Olympic National Park's southern boundary. (Ask rangers about the fording of Success Creek, about 4 miles up the trail.) From Sundown Pass, a high, rough trail leads 2 miles east to Six Ridge Pass (4,650 feet; excellent views), and another 8.5 miles east to a junction with the North Fork Skokomish River Trail. This is a rough alpine traverse. But more than likely, solitude will be easy to come by. Gung-ho day hikers with more stamina than common sense might consider the Colonel Bob Mountain Trail (difficult; 14.6 miles round trip), which departs off South Shore Road, about 6 miles from Highway 101. It climbs quite steeply to an old shelter at 4 miles, then even more steeply to the summit (4,492 feet) and an outstanding view of the Quinault country: lake, valley, peaks, and all. If doing it in a day sounds daunting, good campsites are available along the route for backpackers.

***Boating on the Lake.*** The clear, quiet waters of Lake Quinault are ideal for daylong paddle excursions by kayak or canoe. Willaby and Falls View campgrounds on South Shore Road have good launch areas and day-use parking. Canoes and rowboats can be rented during summer months from Lake Quinault Lodge; 360/288-2571 or 800/562-6672 (from Washington and Oregon only). Other rentals and launch facilities are available a mile up the road at Rain Forest Resort; 360/288-2535.

***Watching Wildlife.*** Lake Quinault is a birder's bonanza. Dozens of aquatic birds drop in or live here year-round, including mallards, loons, and cormorants, and bald eagles make frequent flyovers. Watch for them when kayaking or canoeing, or walking the shoreline portion of the Quinault Loop Trail near Lake Quinault Lodge. The broad floodplains along the river beyond the head of the lake are a primary winter habitat for one of Olympic Park's predominant Roosevelt elk herds. You may see them browsing in the bushes along North Shore Road, between the park's Quinault Ranger Station and the bridge connecting

***At Amanda Park, just north of the turnoff to Lake Quinault Lodge, pause for a stretch and a look at Amanda Park Mercantile. They stock a little bit of everything, including checked flannel loggers' shirts; buy one to wear on your rain-forest hike and feel like a real West Ender.***

RAINFOREST - 1(800) 255-6936

North and South Shore Roads. Along forest trails, watch and listen for winter wrens, kinglets, and juncos.

## LODGINGS

### LAKE QUINAULT LODGE

This massive, cedar-shingled lodge is in the time-honored tradition of great old national park lodges. It sits grandly above the lawns that descend to the lake, with a backdrop of dense evergreen forest. The public rooms are done up like Grandma's sun porch in wicker and antiques, though you may feel you're sitting in a gift shop, with counters filling the entire wall opposite the huge stone fireplace. The dining room overlooks the lawns, and the bar is lively at night. Rooms in the main building are small but perfectly acceptable; half have lake views. Though the adjoining wing has balconies and fireplaces (gas) in each unit, the decor leaves much to be desired; try, instead, to secure one of the 36 newer lakeside rooms, a short walk from the lodge. There are now two handicapped-accessible guest rooms. Amenities and amusements consist of a sauna, an indoor heated pool, a Jacuzzi, a game room, canoes and rowboats, and croquet and volleyball on the lawn. Hiking and running trails are well maintained. Summer reservations call for about two months' advance notice; winter is better, and gives you a chance to experience the true essence of the rain forest. The dining room puts up a classy front, with some evidence of creativity, such as grilled salmon with lingonberry sauce. On occasion there are conventioneers and tour buses around, drawn by the spalike features of the resort, but by and large the old place still exudes the quiet elegance of its past. *PO Box 7, Quinault; South Shore Rd, Quinault; 800/562-6672 (from WA and OR only) or 360/288-2571; $$–$$$; AE, MC, V; checks OK.*

### LAKE QUINAULT RESORT

Longtime Lake Quinault visitors are in awe of what Peggy and Ed Backholm have created from an aged motel on the lake's north shore. The resort, surrounded by forests on three sides and with the lake straight ahead, consists of five one-story rooms, completely redone, and three new two-story units. All share a wide deck provided with Adirondack chairs and lavished with flower-filled planters. There's nothing between you and that bewitching lake—unless an eagle flies by. The one-story units have kitchenettes, one or two bedrooms and baths with shower; one preserves the original knotty pine walls. The two-story townhouse suites have a sitting area and bed and bath downstairs, another bedroom upstairs. They're spiffy and equipped with a small refrigerator, microwave, coffeepot, and toaster—no sink or utensils. In all units, the TV hides in an armoire. Though just lounging on the lawn and gazing dreamily at the lake is heavenly, if conviviality's your thing, you may join other guests at a campfire, and a gas barbecue and a gazebo are available for outdoor gatherings (but quiet time starts at 10). The Backholms will advise on explorations into the rain forest or out to ocean beaches. *314 N Shore Rd, Amanda Park; 2 miles east of Hwy 101 on N Shore Rd; 800/650-2362 or 360/288-2362; www.lakequinault.com; $$–$$$; AE, DIS, MC, V; checks OK.*

## LOCHAERIE RESORT ☆

View Drive Lake Quinault's North Shore Road 4 miles to this away-from-it-all resort, a cluster of six endearing cabins scattered down a steepish slope to the lake (bring your flashlight). The first cabins were built in 1926, but even the newer ones manage to achieve the same aging-gracefully look. All are named for Olympic peaks; they sleep two to six persons. Angeles, near the top and recently renovated, sleeps two. Colonel Bob, the largest and newest, is near the beach and sleeps six. Christie, most in demand and down the most steps, sleeps three. It perches on Onion Rock, with spectacular views of the lake and mountains. All have fireplaces, and linens and kitchen utensils are provided. Firewood is free, and so are guests' use of the canoes on the beach and views of otters sunning on the float. Still no TV or phones—in fact nothing much has changed here for years, except the pet policy: now they are allowed, for $25 each. *638 N Shore Rd, Amanda Park; 4 miles east of Hwy 101 on N Shore Rd; 360/288-2215; www.lochaerie.com, $; no credit cards; checks OK.*

***Lake Quinault Resort's enticements include a cruise. Twice a day, morning and evening, their lakeworthy little vessel sets out from the beach below the lodge on a one-hour voyage all around the lake. It's worth the $5 per head, as you marvel at rare old-growth forest (one of the last surviving stands), see where the Quinault Tribe are successfully rearing salmon, and watch a row of cormorants on a log spread their wings to dry. Looking uplake at forested hills backdropped by snowclad peaks, you could imagine yourself cruising an Alaska fjord—it's that pure and remote.***

# CENTRAL COAST

*Taholah, the northernmost town of South Beach, is the home of the Quinault Nation, and has access to some of the south coast's most spectacular beaches. But don't trespass—stop at tribal headquarters in town to get permission to walk the beach.*

From Moclips south to Tokeland, the Washington coastline varies from rocky beaches to long expanses of sand, from working harbors and mill towns to muddy tideflats and bird sanctuaries. Highway 101 leaves the coast at Queets, but less prominent—and often more pleasant—thoroughfares provide easy access to the beaches and bays of the central Washington coast. Highway 109 runs along the shoreline and Pacific beaches between the Quinault Reservation and Aberdeen, while Highway 105 bends around the southern side of Grays Harbor and wends its way to Raymond and South Bend. Two narrow peninsulas guard the entrance to Grays Harbor. On the northern one are the windswept sand dunes and glitzy resorts of popular Ocean Shores. On the southern point is Westport, favorite destination of sports fishers. For quieter retreats, explore the estuaries and tidelands around Grayland and Tokeland.

## NORTH BEACH

The area between Taholah and Ocean Shores is known as North Beach. The beaches between Taholah, headquarters of the Quinault Indian Nation, and Moclips are closed to the public, but there are plenty of accessible stretches farther south, and a row of small towns catering to beachhounds: Moclips, Pacific Beach, Copalis Beach, and Ocean City. Toward the north, beaches are more rocky and spectacular; toward the south, sandier and broader. In razor-clam season, booted, bucket-bearing diggers throng the shores.

## ACTIVITIES

***Smoked Salmon.*** For a tasty souvenir, pick up a gift pack from the fish cannery of the Quinault Indian Nation, available at the general store in Taholah or at shops up and down the peninsula (or by mail from PO Box 217, Taholah, WA 98587). You can choose a 5-ounce package of smoked salmon, or splurge on a wooden box of assorted delicacies.

***Java, Muffins, and Kites.*** A coffee stop at the very casual Granitas Breakfast & Bakery at the crossroads in Ocean City

(2 Second Avenue) is more than a shot of java. Have a fresh-baked muffin or slice of pizza and relax inside or at a picnic table outside, where you can revel in the fresh salt air. Buy a kite and head for the beach.

***Take the Pooch to the Shore.*** Drive down Banner Road in Copalis Beach, and at the end stop at Griffiths Priday State Park, a handy rest stop for you, your dog, and the kids. There are picnic tables, restaurants, and a wide-open expanse of grassy area to run about and play Frisbee. The ocean is just over the dunes.

***Copalis Beach claims to sit at the north end of the world's greatest razor-clam bed. During the clam seasons (spring and fall), the hamlet's normal population of 350 is quadrupled. You need a state license ($7) and you can rent shovels and clam guns in local shops. For information on seasons and safety, call the Westport-Grayland Chamber of Commerce, 800/345-6223 or 360/268-9422; or e-mail them, westport@techline.com***

## LODGINGS

### IRON SPRINGS RESORT ☆

This four-decades-old resort is on one of the most satisfying beaches on the peninsula. Twenty-eight cabins dot the slope from blufftop to creekside, sited so everybody has an ocean view. Most have fireplaces. Older cottages have recently been completely updated, and nearly all have been refurnished; no TVs, but you can rent one here or bring your portable. Privacy is paramount, and spruce trees and fences form a screen between neighbors. Larger two-bedroom cottages sleep up to 11; the others sleep 2 to 4. The two studio apartments in the reception building are the least expensive, and even they have a view of the river and a slice of ocean. Take a swim in the covered, heated pool. Buy some of longtime owner Olive Little's yummy cinnamon rolls. Take the nature walk with the ocean overlook, or the woodsy one along the creek. Hike the beach, comb it for agates, shells, and driftwood, or go crabbing or clamming on the resort's 2,000 feet of ocean front. *PO Box 207, Copalis Beach; Hwy 109, 3 miles north of Copalis Beach; 360/276-4230; www.ironspringsresort.com; $; AE, D, MC, V; checks OK.*

### MOONSTONE BEACH MOTEL

It's modest in every respect except color: a row of eight little motel units that look as though they've been painted with orange sherbet, a few yards north of the bridge into Moclips. Between you and the ocean, there's nothing but a veranda with seen-better-days lounge chairs and picnic tables. Second-floor guests see a little more sea. All units have kitchens (though not necessarily ovens), and there's a separate six-person cabin. Good razor clamming and drift-wood browsing. Plan ahead, as this place fills up fast for the summer. *4849 Pacific St, PO Box 156, Moclips; 30 miles north of Ocean Shores; 888/888-9063 or 360/276-4346; www.wpshopper.com/moonstone.html; $; MC, V; checks OK.*

### OCEAN CREST RESORT ☆

View Nestled in a magnificent stand of spruce on a bluff high above one of the nicest stretches of beach on the Olympic Peninsula, the Ocean Crest has always offered rooms with memorable views. The best views now are those from the modern units—done up in cedar paneling with fireplaces and European-style showers—and the best of the best are in Building 5. A recreation center is just across the road, with a swimming pool, sauna, Jacuzzi, and weight room, and there's access to the beach along a winding walkway through a lovely wooded ravine. An annex a quarter-mile down the road offers two apartments, each with complete kitchen, porch, and two bedrooms. There are few prospects on the Northwest coast that can rival the panorama from the dining room at the Ocean Crest, but unfortunately the food and service do not live up to the view. Upstairs is a cozy bar, furnished with Northwest Coast Indian artifacts. *PO Box 7, Moclips; 18 miles north of Ocean Shores; 800/684-8439 or 360/276-4465; $$$; AE, MC, V; checks OK.*

### SAND DOLLAR INN

View The new owners have done a commendable job of remodeling this 50-year-old two-story-plus-penthouse motel. It's just 200 feet from the dunes and many rooms have ocean views. The seven motel rooms are bright and airy, simply but pleasingly furnished, with one or two bedrooms and all but one with a kitchen. Those upstairs have access to a deck. Guests are welcome to use the fenced garden patio in back, a nice suntrap, with barbecue and hot tub. Rates are reasonable, and for a very little more you may engage the penthouse with its huge picture windows and the best view of all.

Several neat shingled cottages across the street have one or two bedrooms, a living room, and full kitchen; nice for families. The largest cabin sleeps six and has a fenced yard; for another five bucks, bring your pet. *53 Central Ave, PO Box 206, Pacific Beach; 2nd and Central; 360/276-4525; sandlrin@techline.com; $$; MC, V; checks OK.*

### SANDPIPER BEACH RESORT ★★

A longtime tradition for beachhounds, this is the place to bring the kids, the grandparents, and the family dog. It's right on the beach and consists of two four-story complexes containing large, fully equipped suites—usually a sitting room with a dining area and a fireplace, a compact kitchen including a microwave, a small porch, and a bedroom and bath. There are splendid views of the beach (and a children's play area) from every deck. Penthouse units have an extra bedroom and cathedral ceilings. There are also one-room studios, and five older cottages. This resort knows enough not to try to compete with the draws of the Pacific: there's no pool, no TV, no restaurant, no in-room telephones, no video machines—but the large gift shop does sell board games, kites, and sand buckets, plus condiments and sportswear. The only bow to the times is an espresso bar. Prices are reasonable and the staff is very hospitable. Minimum stays are imposed on all weekends and in the summer, and reservations are best made months in advance. Housekeeping drops by every day to see if you need anything (but you'll need to pay extra for logs for the fireplace); otherwise you're on your own—just like home. *4159 Hwy 109, PO Box A, Pacific Beach; 1½ miles south of Pacific Beach; 800/567-4737 or 360/276-4580; sandpiper@techline.com; www.sandpiper-resort.com; $$; MC, V; checks OK.*

## OCEAN SHORES

Born as a real-estate promoter's dream in 1970, this 6,000-acre, 6-mile-long peninsula is finally outgrowing its schlocky past. The push for big-time gambling has waned (though there are rumors of a casino) and the convention center is busy year-round with trade shows, collectors' fairs, and art exhibits. There's an annual

***There are almost as many ways to get help from the Ocean Shores Chamber of Commerce as there are grains of sand on the beach. By phone, 800/76-BEACH or 360/289-2451; by fax, 360/289-0226; by mail, PO Box 382, Ocean Shores; by e-mail, oschamber@ coastaccess.com.; or visit their website, www. oceanshores.org; or drop in at their office, 120 West Chance a la Mer Boulevard.***

jazz festival, a photography show with a statewide following, and sand-castle and kite-flying competitions. McDonald's put up its golden arches in 1994 and building is booming. If you came here to get away from it all, a good way to avoid downtown altogether is to reserve one of the private beach houses and condominiums that owners occasionally rent. Reservations need to be made weeks in advance; 800/562-8612 or 360/289-3941. The early entrepreneurs did us all a favor when they dredged 10 miles of freshwater canals into the center of the peninsula, as well as Duck Lake—long, slender, and dotted with islands.

## ACTIVITIES

***The Lure of the Lake.*** Dazed by the long, well-developed beaches on the west side, Ocean Shores visitors are often glad to discover Duck Lake, a relatively unspoiled body of water, ideal for boating, fishing, and water skiing. Take your binoculars; waterfowl gather here, and deer and raccoons are in residence. "Duck Lake is like a Monet every morning," says an Ocean Shores resident who visits it daily.

***Boat Rentals.*** Summer Sails and Rentals (on Grand Canal, 952 Point Brown Avenue SE; 360/289-2884) will rent you a canoe or a powerboat by the hour for your Duck Lake pleasures. Life jackets are provided. Bass and trout await your line. Or go canoeing or kayaking in the canals.

***Natural History.*** At the Environmental Interpretive Center, run by the city of Ocean Shores, displays will give you a quick course in the peninsula's geologic and natural history—good prep for your beachcombing and bird-watching. Open daily in summer, some weekends in winter (call first). At the end of Point Brown Avenue; 360/289-4617.

***Over the Waves to Westport.*** At the south end of the Ocean Shores peninsula and near the marina, the passenger ferry *Matador* makes round-trips to Westport: six trips daily in summer, reduced schedule spring and fall, no service in winter. It's a great convenience for bikers, day-trippers, and travelers overnighting in either location. A trolley shuttles passengers between central Ocean Shores and the dock, and the pier in

Westport is on Westhaven Avenue, close to everything. Tickets and information at 2453 Westhaven Drive, Float 10, Westport; 360/268-0047.

***Gallop the Beach.*** Step outside your room at Best Western Lighthouse Suites Inn and you're practically on a horse's back. Chenois Creek Horse Rentals are right there on the beach at the end of Damon Road. Only have half an hour? That's just $10; an hour is $15. 360/533-5591; chenoiscreek@techline.com; www.oceanshores.org. Ask at the Chamber of Commerce about other horse rentals.

***Golf the Coast.*** Between Duck Lake and the Grand Canal, Ocean Shores Golf Course is billed as the only championship 18-hole golf course on the Washington coast (500 Canal Drive NE; 360/289-3357).

***Shop.*** How refreshing: a noncutesy gift shop in a place that revels in kitsch. Gallery Marjuli sells unusual stationery, art prints, glass, and original Northwest paintings. Just through the Ocean Shores gate, at 865 Point Brown Avenue NW; 360/289-2855.

## RESTAURANTS

### ALEC'S BY THE SEA ☆

Alec's by the Sea is a friendly family restaurant that does a lot of things well, including grilled razor clams, chicken fettuccine, and steaks. The delicious Philadelphia Prime Sandwich features sliced prime rib, grilled with onions and juicy bell peppers, topped with Swiss cheese, and served on a toasted French roll. The menu is large, portions are generous, the waitstaff is efficient, and crayons are offered for kids. *131 E Chance a la Mer Blvd NE; Point Brown Rd, left onto Chance a la Mer Blvd NE; 360/289-4026; $$; DC, MC, V; local checks only; lunch, dinner every day; full bar.*

### GALWAY BAY RESTAURANT & PUB

Guinness (which everyone *knows* is good for you) is on tap, and also an ingredient in many of the allegedly authentic Emerald Isle dishes (which include a corned beef pizza).

This is the place to warm up after a day of beachcombing. There's a jolly family atmosphere, with Irish reels playing in the background. *676 Ocean Shores Blvd NW, Ocean Shores; in town on Nantucket Square, half a block from Shilo Inn; 360/289-2300; $$; AE, DC, MC, V; checks OK; lunch, dinner every day; full bar.* ♿

## LODGINGS

### THE BEST WESTERN LIGHTHOUSE SUITES INN ★

View This handsome, hospitable hotel is one of the better places to stay on the beach. Each tastefully decorated, spacious room features a fireplace, wet bar, microwave, refrigerator, and coffeepot, plus cable TV and VCR. Sixty of the 76 rooms have a full ocean view. There's an indoor pool and spa and a cozy library. No restaurant, but a continental breakfast is free.*491 Damon Rd NW, PO Box 879, Ocean Shores; at the north city limits; 800/757-SURF or 360/289-2311; 1757surf@techline.com; www.oceanshores.com/lodging/lighthouse; $$$; AE, DC, MC, V; checks OK.* ♿

### THE GRAY GULL ★

View This condominium-resort looks rather like a ski lodge, with jagged angles, handsome cladding, and a front door to strain the mightiest triceps. There are 36 condominium units, facing the ocean at a broad stretch of the beach (though not all have views; prices are calibrated accordingly). Each is outfitted with a balcony, fireplace, kitchen, TV, VCR, and attractive furnishings. The resort has a pool, a sauna, and a spa. You are right on the beach, the main plus. Prices for the suites get fairly steep, but you may save money by cooking in the full kitchen. *651 Ocean Shores Blvd SW, PO Box 1417, Ocean Shores; in town near the Shilo Inn on Ocean Shores Blvd; 800/562-9712 or 360/289-3381; greygull@thegreygull.com; www.thegreygull.com; $$$; AE, DC, MC, V; checks OK.*

### SHILO INN ★★

View The service is first-class at the area's newest, $10-million, 113-suite convention resort. And it's one of the few oceanfront establishments to have lived up to all of its PR hoo-ha. Each of the suites (*all* the rooms are junior suites) features a beachfront balcony (*all* face the ocean), fireplace, microwave, refrigerator, wet bar—everything right down to an iron and ironing board. Facilities include an indoor pool, sauna, steam room, and fitness center. Even the restaurant, with ocean views of course, is a find—with individual pizzas and fresh seafood. Weekend brunches are knockouts. *707 Ocean Shores Blvd NW, Ocean Shores; in town on Ocean Shores Blvd; 800/222-2244 or 360/289-4600; www.shiloinn.com; $$$; AE, DC, MC, V; checks OK.*

## GRAYS HARBOR

The Grays Harbor area is bouncing back from its temporary funk, when its longtime mainstays—timber, salmon, and shipping—declined. Now the appeal of the vast bay, the wilderness backcountry, and the miles of sandy beach brings tourists, retirees, surfers, clam-diggers, and wildlife watchers. There are real-estate bargains galore and a host of lures for the vacationer in the surrounding small towns, including accommodations from historic bed-and-breakfast inns to seaside cabins.

***Cheer on your favorite pony at the horse races at the Grays Harbor County Fair, every August in Elma. It's a good old county fair, with rides, music, dancing, and scrubbed and brushed farm animals on display.***

## ABERDEEN-HOQUIAM

With the timber industry in slow decline, these old Siamese-twin lumber towns on the north shore of Grays Harbor are in transition, as they have been since the sawmilling and shipping glory days of the early 1900s. Lately, with an eye toward tourism, the two towns have been making the most of their nautical history, and the restaurant scene keeps brightening.

### ACTIVITIES

***Where to Stay, Where to Eat?*** Information about the Grays Harbor area is available from the Grays Harbor Chamber of Commerce, 506 Duffy Street, Aberdeen; 800/321-1924 or 360/532-1924; gchamber@techline.com; www.chamber.grays-harbor.wa.us. It's between the eastbound and westbound thoroughfares, near the Health Department. They're up to date on accommodations, dining, and the sailing plans of the *Lady*

*Washington.* Or get in touch with Tourism Grays Harbor, PO Box 225, Aberdeen; 800/621-9625 or 360/533-7895; tourism@graysharbor.com; www.graysharbor.com.

***Pause for a bit of history and a garden stroll at the Polson Museum in Hoquiam. It's housed in a fine home built for F. Arnold Polson in 1923, and filled with memorabilia of Grays Harbor's logging heyday. The surrounding small park has a charming rose garden; 1611 Riverside Avenue, Hoquiam; 360/533-5862.***

***Birds on the Beach.*** At the tidal mudflats of Bowerman Basin, a half-million shorebirds make a rest and feeding stop during spring and fall migrations and bird-watchers flock to the beach to watch. Some two dozen bird species visit, including sandpipers, dowitchers, and dunlins. Best viewing time is an hour before high tide, mid-April through the first week of May. Few who have seen it can forget the heart-stopping sight as the birds rise in unison in thick flocks that shimmer through the air, twisting and turning, before settling back onto their feeding grounds. Keep your distance—remember these birds are feeding as hard as they can for the long journey to come, and the least human disturbance can drive them from their dinner. Heading north out of Hoquiam on Highway 109, look for the sign to the airport and follow the airport road to trail signs to the beach. Trails are almost certain to be muddy, so wear boots. For more information on access and peak migratory days, call the Grays Harbor Chamber of Commerce, 800/321-1924 or 360/532-1924; or the Nisqually National Wildlife Refuge Complex, 360/753-9467.

***River Kayaking.*** It could be the highlight of your Olympic Peninsula experience: kayaking one or more of the seven rivers that flow into Grays Harbor. With Resonance Canoe & Kayak (409 E Market, Aberdeen; 360/532-9176) you can not only paddle along nearby rivers, but out in Willapa Bay or on Lake Quinault in the rain forest. Travel with one of their guides for $50 for 2½ hours, $70 for a whole day, including lunch. Life vests are provided. Get the whole story at www.resonance.cc, or e-mail them at makewaves@olypen.com.

***Sail into the Past.*** Aberdeen's pride and joy is the splendid replica of Captain Gray's *Lady Washington,* a 105-foot, 170-ton tall ship, as seaworthy as the 1787 original. With the temporary demise of the Grays Harbor Historical Seaport, she is now moored across the river—call 800/200-LADY to find her. Dockside tours are available ($3 adults, $2 seniors and students, $1 children under 12). Or hop aboard the ship for a three-hour sail of Grays Harbor or the Chehalis River ($35 adults, $15 children).

The *Lady* will also welcome you to join the crew for longer sails throughout Puget Sound, your chance to stand a trick at the tiller or haul away at a halyard; ports of call include Gig Harbor, Port Townsend, Tacoma, and points north. For reservations and information, call 800/200-LADY or 360/532-8611.

***For the full small-town experience, take yourself out to the ball game and yell for the home team. The Grays Harbor Gulls have decamped, but the Rain team plays on. The ballfield is at the historic Olympic Stadium (Cherry and 28th in west Aberdeen), one of the few wood stadia still standing—it's been there since 1915. Get schedules at the Grays Harbor Chamber of Commerce.***

***Lumber Baron Luxury.*** To see how the lumber barons lived, tour Hoquiam's Castle, a 20-room, three-story mansion built by prominent lumberman Robert Lytle in 1897 (515 Chenault Avenue, Hoquiam; 360/533-2005). Among the marvels: a 3,000-pound 1897 pool table with cast-iron lions for legs that had to be hoisted up to the top floor and maneuvered through the windows. Right next door is the equally splendid house Lytle's brother built—now the Lytle House Bed and Breakfast (see Lodgings).

***Take a Cue.*** Drop into Book Carnival (219 E Wishkah Street; 360/533-4070), a pool hall where you'll find a terrific variety of magazines for sale: not only every hunting and fishing magazine in the land, but also *Atlantic Monthly, Discover,* and *Mother Jones.*

***Curtain Now Going Up.*** Hoquiam's once-resplendent 7th Street Theater has regained its true glory, after many years of volunteer effort. Its stage presents touring performers, local amateur productions, and performances by the 7th Street Kids—actors are children but it's fun for all ages. The theater is a splendid sight, worth a look even if you can't stay; on 7th Street between K and L. Ask the Chamber of Commerce for a list of upcoming events. 800/321-1924 or 360/532-1924.

## RESTAURANTS

***Parma Fans Advisory:*** At press time, Pierre Gabelli, owner and chef of Parma's in Aberdeen (116 W Heron; 360/532-3166) was planning to pull up stakes and move to "somewhere on Bainbridge Island," where he will con-tinue to serve up his delectable and original cuisine. The Aberdeen restaurant will remain, but under new ownership and with a new name.

### BILLY'S BAR & GRILL ★

The best little whorehouse in town used to be right across the street from this historic pub, and the walls at Billy's sport some original artwork that recalls Aberdeen's bawdy past. The place is named after the infamous Billy Gohl, who terrorized the Aberdeen waterfront in 1907. Billy shanghaied sailors and robbed loggers, consigning their bodies to the murky Wishkah River through a trapdoor in a saloon only a block away from the present-day Billy's—where you get a square-deal meal (thick burgers and ranch fries, oyster shooters for under a dollar, and a good old meat-loaf dinner) and an honest drink without much damage to your pocketbook. Green-shaded lamps, red leather booths, and the long, substantial, well-stocked bar make you want to linger. *322 E Heron St, Aberdeen; corner of Heron and G; 360/533-7144; $; AE, DC, MC, V; local checks only; lunch, dinner every day; full bar.* ♿

### BRIDGES ★

Sonny Bridges started out with a corner cafe over 30 years ago and kept expanding his horizons—both in space and in taste. You'll find yourself in an airy, pastel-hued setting with lots of cozy corners and an amazingly eclectic collection of books. The diverse menu contains few surprises, but Sonny owns a piece of the best seafood market in town, and the clams and salmon can't be beat. There's also prime rib that's really prime and pasta that hasn't been overcooked. Burnt cream is their dessert specialty. The busy bar is first-class, with Northwest wines, beers, espresso drinks, and grilled oysters. The staff, as always, is extraordinarily professional. *112 N G St, Aberdeen; 1st and G; 360/532-6563; $$; AE, DC, MC, V; local checks only; lunch Mon–Sat, dinner every day; full bar.* ♿

## LODGINGS

### ABERDEEN MANSION INN ★★

It's a bit of a tourist attraction, what with street signs leading from downtown to this "historic Aberdeen mansion" and tours for a fee. But if you get beyond that and actually make a reservation, your stay will be pleasant, peaceful, and private. Michael and Karen Pavlevich turned the local landmark into a charming four-bedroom bed-and-breakfast inn. For families, the Pavleviches have created a small apartment over the garage, the Carriage House, with a minikitchen and sleeping accommodations for three or four. *807 N M St, Aberdeen; corner of 5th; 888/533-7079 or 360/533-7079; joanw@techline.com; www.techline.com/~joanw/; $$–$$$; AE, DIS, MC, V; checks OK.*

***Take a break as you drive through Hoquiam on a rainy day: stop at the Timberland Library (621 K Street), sit a spell by the fire, and find the answers to those questions that have been nagging you. Chairs and a sofa curl around the fireplace, and shelves of reference books flank the chimney.***

## COONEY MANSION ☆☆

Cosmopolis, the oldest town on Grays Harbor, was born and reared in the heyday of the timber industry. Tycoon Neil Cooney built this mansion in 1910 to showcase his mill's products. For many years he lived here, lord of the manor, and entertained his out-of-town guests. There's a very masculine feel to the place (Cooney was a bachelor and a J. Edgar Hoover–style taskmaster who had 1,200 workers under his thumb): spruce wainscoting in the living room, large windows with dark wooden frames, heavy Craftsman furniture throughout. From the deck on the second floor you can sit and watch golfers on the 18-hole public course next door. Tennis courts are visible as you head up the driveway (they are part of Mill Creek Park, but are available for guests' use). For duck watchers, Mill Creek Park at the bottom of the hill has winding paths through the trees and along the stream. After your game or walk, visit the sauna and whirlpool in the basement of the mansion. Jim and Judi Lohr are fastidious hosts, offering eight guest rooms, four with double, queen, or king beds and private baths; the others share baths. A bounteous Lumber Baron's Breakfast comes with the room. *1705 5th St, Cosmopolis; follow C St to 5th and drive up hill to end; 360/533-0602; cooney@techline.com; $$; AE, DIS, MC, V; no checks.*

## LYTLE HOUSE BED & BREAKFAST ☆

In 1897, when timber baron Robert Lytle built what was to become Hoquiam's architectural landmark, Hoquiam's Castle, his brother Joseph erected a smaller version next door. This has become Lytle House, decorated with the almost requisite Victorian embellishments throughout, including a magnificent square grand piano. The front parlor feels too formal for hunkering down in a big chair with a book, but there are more than enough parlors for all, some more cozy. The eight guest rooms, six with private baths, are quite spacious. On the second floor the Windsor Room has a small library, an antique woodstove, and a balcony overlooking the town, the lush lawn, and flower beds. Two rooms have huge claw-foot tubs. Excellent breakfasts include granola, yogurt, fresh fruit, and omelets. Owners Robert and Dayna Bencala—two young refugees from California—are B&B hosts of the best kind: genuinely hospitable yet unobtrusive. If you insist on bringing your work with you, there are in-room phones and a fax machine. *509 Chenault, Hoquiam; west on Emerson, right on Garfield, up hill to Chenault; 800/677-2320 or 360/533-2320; benchmark@ techline; $$; MC, V; checks OK.*

## MONTESANO

County seat of historically rich Grays Harbor County, Montesano is just off Highway 112, 15 miles east of Aberdeen. Drive up First Street for the full effect of the 90-year-old county courthouse—a pillared, clock-towered, sandstone structure that dominates the town. Inside the building, an awesome marble staircase is flanked by murals of Captain Robert Gray discovering Grays Harbor and Governor Isaac Stevens treating with the Indians. A stroll around this part of town will reveal a number of fine old homes, built at the end of the last century. According to one story, Montesano's name comes from the Spanish for "mountain health," and a drive up primitive roads through national forest land will indeed lead to some healthy mountains: the southern Olympics, with relatively unpeopled parks along the way.

### RESTAURANTS

#### SAVORY FAIRE ★★

Marvelous aromas come wafting out of Candi and Randy Bachtell's fetching little restaurant, just a block down the street from the courthouse. Breakfasts feature flawlessly cooked omelets, country-fried potatoes, fresh-baked breads, and wonderful cinnamon rolls. The coffee is superb. At lunchtime, try the turkey pesto sandwich or an exceptional French dip on garlic-rosemary bread. There's a wine boutique on the premises with a good selection of regional wines and naturally brewed beers, as well as specialty coffees, cookbooks, condiments, and kitchenware. Eat inside (closer to the appetizing aromas) or on the suntrap of a patio, centered on a little pool and surrounded by flowers and shrubbery. *135 S Main St, Montesano; take Montesano exit off Hwy 12, drive uphill on Main St; 360/249-3701; $; AE, MC, V; checks OK; breakfast, lunch Mon–Sat; beer and wine.*

***Enjoy a side trip from Montesano to Lake Sylvia State Park, about a mile north of town. It's just the place for a picnic, a fishing break, or an overnight. You'll find a boat launch, boat rentals, wooded campsites, and handicapped-accessible nature trails. For information, call 360/249-3621.***

## LODGINGS

### ABEL HOUSE ★

Jerry and Beth Reeves came to the rescue of this magnificent old home, built in 1908 by William Abel, a prominent Montesano attorney, and updated it just enough but not too much. The finely crafted woodwork gleams, old-fashioned roses perfume the gardens, and the elevator is back in service. Hospitality is generous: Beth, with the help of her mother and sister, prepares a full country breakfast that could include waffles, sausage, pancakes, or a Monte Cristo sandwich. As though that weren't enough, an elegantly presented complimentary afternoon tea is served on the veranda or in the dining room. And as if *that* weren't enough, you're treated to a bedtime snack—fruit, cookies, even a glass of wine. The third-floor game room is fitted with pool and Ping-Pong tables, piano, TV, and VCR. You're also invited to play the baby grand piano in the parlor, have a go at croquet or badminton on the lawn, or borrow a bike. The bedrooms are charming and spotless: the Abel Suite has a view of the courthouse, a king bed, private bath, and elevator access, and the other four rooms have king, queen, or twin beds, and share three baths. Children are welcome, and cribs and rollaways available. *117 Fleet St S, Montesano; north on Main St, left on Pioneer Ave W to Fleet St; 360/249-6002; $$; AE, DC, DIS, MC, V; checks OK.*

## WESTPORT

*Once a year, Brady's Oysters in Westport takes pity on the oyster-starved and schedules a season for U-pickers at the company's own beds. For schedules, call 800/572-3252.*

For a small coastal town that regularly endures flood tides of tourists, Westport remains surprisingly friendly, scenic, and uncondominiumed. Most fishers rise early and join the almost comically hasty 6am exodus from the breakwater to cross the bumpy bar and head for the open sea. The unpredictable salmon fishing seasons of recent years have changed charter-boat marketing. Bottom-fishing trips for halibut, lingcod, and rockfish are increasingly popular, and many charter operators now feature bird-watching and whale-watching cruises as well. Gray whales migrate off the coast March through May on their way toward Arctic feeding waters, where they fatten up for the trip back down to their breeding lagoons in Baja come fall. Breakfast cafes are open by 5am, some much earlier (especially those down by the docks).

*For bed and board as you enter Westport, look for clean, burgundy-trimmed Mariner's Cove Inn, set back from the road at 303 Ocean Avenue; 360/268-0531. Two units have kitchenettes; there's a gazebo for picnics. Next door is Bakery Cottage, a cozy cafe where everything's baked fresh daily.*

## ACTIVITIES

***Bivalves and Bangers.*** You can drop by and pick up a bushel of Brady's Oysters (turn right on Oyster Place, just south of the bridge as you come into town on Highway 105)—or other choice seafoods, such as a can of smoked oysters or a halibut steak for your dinner. Or stop at nearby Bay City Sausage Company, 2249 Highway 105, and take home some great beef jerky, chorizo, kielbasa, cranberry-turkey sausage, or any of about 45 other kinds of sausage, made on the premises.

***Fishing Charters.*** Charter rates vary little from company to company. Some of the best charters include Cachalot, 360/268-0323; Deep Sea, 800/562-0151 or 360/268-9300; Westport, 800/562-0157 or 360/268-9120; Islander, 800/322-1740 or 360/268-9166; Coho Charters, 800/572-0177 or 360/268-0111; Washington Charters, 800/562-0173 or 360/268-0900; Salmon Charters, 800/562-0157; and Travis, 360/268-9140. (Toll-free numbers may not be in operation during the winter.)

***Exploring.*** Things quiet down until the 3:30pm return of the fleets. You can explore the town during this lull, and walk the waterfront promenade with its parade of exhibits of historic ships that have sunk or swum along this stretch of the coast. At the south end of Westhaven Drive, a climb up the viewing tower affords a fine view of the harbor, the sea, and if you're lucky, a breaching whale.

***Beaches.*** All the beaches to the south are open for driving, jogging, clamming, or picnicking. At Westhaven State Park, a short drive or bike ride from Westport, a concrete walkway crests the dunes all the way to the historic Westport Lighthouse—the tallest in Washington State. From an observation platform, watch for ships and whales and, on a clear day, maybe a glimpse of Mt. Olympus. Wet-suited surfers can be found year-round near the South Jetty, which traps incoming southwesterly waves, hoping to catch their own Big One. Caution to beach drivers: The sand along Westhaven Beach is very soft. Caution to beach walkers: Be alert for beach drivers exceeding the 25-mph limit.

***Seafood with a View.*** Pelican Point, the teal-blue eatery at the end of Westhaven Drive (2681 Westhaven Drive; 360/268-1333) is a popular spot for seafood and steaks. Dine on the deck, or inside; either way, you have good views of the spirited marina. Breakfast, lunch and dinner, Tuesday through Sunday.

***Nautical History, Nantucket Style.*** Westport's Maritime Museum is housed in a former Coast Guard station that would look at home on Cape Cod, with its three stories, six gables, and widow's walk. It's worth a stop if for no more than a gander at the architecture. Besides a thorough look at the area's history, centered on whaling, fishing, and cranberries, the museum presents in an annex a giant Fresnel lens from the Destruction Island lighthouse that rotates before goggle-eyed watchers like a prismatic light show. The museum (2201 Westhaven Drive; 360/268-0078) is open Wednesday through Sunday, spring and summer.

## LODGINGS

### THE CHATEAU WESTPORT ☆

The Chateau is considered the fanciest motel lodging in Westport, though it bears no resemblance to any chateau we know. Prices for the 108 condo-style units are moderate, especially in the off-season, when the beachcombing is the best; an indoor pool and hot tub are available, and there's volleyball on the back lawn. Studio units have fireplaces and can be rented alone (with a queen-size hideabed) or in conjunction with adjoining bedrooms to form a suite. It's not the quietest place, and the continental breakfast is nothing to get excited about, but the ocean views are magnificent; those from the third and fourth floors are best. No pets. *710 W Hancock, Westport; Hancock and S Forrest Sts; 800/255-9101 or 360/268-9101; $$; AE, DC, MC, V; no checks.*

### GLENACRES INN

Turn-of-the-century entrepreneuse Minnie Armstrong ran a horse 'n' buggy service from the docks of Westport to her bed-and-breakfast long before B&Bs became the latest thing in overnight accommodations. The trees are taller now (so you don't have a sense of the ocean) but the place is still a gabled gem with lots of lodging alternatives on its 9 acres. In addition to the five bedrooms in the inn there are three simpler "deck" rooms in an ell off the main building—these have adjoining doors so two or three can be rented by families. Children are welcome in these rooms and in the two cottages with kitchens, which new owners Pat Walker and Linda Drais are busy renovating. There's a hot tub in a gazebo on the back deck. Prices are reasonable, and guests in the main inn are served a tasty Continental breakfast. *222 N Montesano, PO Box 1246, Westport; 1 block north of the stoplight on N Montesano; 360/268-9391; $; MC, V; checks OK.*

### HARBOR RESORT

Way out at the end of the jetty, Mark Dodson runs this modest but appealing resort: a general store with lodgings upstairs, a row of sea-facing cottages, and fishing and whale-watching packages. Crabbing brings many, and Mark rents crab traps, educates fledgling crabbers, and steers them to likely spots along the docks. A tiny restaurant at the back of the store offers clam chowder, Grandpa Ed's Chili, steamed clams, and of course crab. Whales sometimes come right into Westport Harbor and can be spied from the resort's ocean-facing rooms—also sea otters. Mark has classed up the modest rooms in the store building with nautical touches and period furnishings. Some have kitchens, all have private baths, and some with adjoining doors can be rented as a suite. Three rooms look straight out toward the sunset and Tokyo; the others view the marina. The five new, boxy cottages with decks over the water sleep four; they're nicely furnished and have kitchens, TVs, and plenty of privacy; some have Jacuzzis. *871 Neddie Rose Dr, Westport; at end of Westhaven Dr turn right onto Neddie Rose; 360/268-0169; www.harborresort.com; $–$$; AE, D, MC, V; no checks.*

## GRAYLAND

Along Highway 105's ocean stretch, two wonderful, uncrowded beaches extend for miles. At Twin Harbors State Park, 2 miles south of Westport, you'll find a nature trail winding through the dunes, campsites, a playground, and more than 3 miles of ocean beach. Grayland Beach State Park has similar attractions, as well as a self-guided nature tour that takes you through pine and spruce forest.

## ACTIVITIES

***Crazy about Cranberries.*** From Grayland south is cranberry country; bogs east of Highway 105 produce most of Washington's cranberries. Grayland has a Cranberry Harvest Festival in the fall, when berries are ripe and the bogs are a sea of brilliant red. The festival features bog tours, incredible varieties of cranberry edibles, a Cranberry Cook-off, live music, and a parade through Grayland. Call 800/473-6018 for more information.

***Omelet Stop.*** At Golden Cove Omelettes (2021 Highway 105, Grayland; 360/267-1034), breakfast is served all day, hardly enough time to choose among the 64 kinds of omelets, from peanut-butter-and-jelly to ground sirloin with tomatoes and scallions. The fish and chips are a sure-fire winner, and you might want to try eggs Benedict with crab instead of ham, served with a pair of crab legs on the side. Crack and pick while you look out across salt meadows and an RV park to the sea.

***Stroll a mile down the road from the Tokeland Hotel to the very tip of the peninsula, a peaceful spot where the crab boats hang out at the well-weathered marina. Look across the bay to the tip of the Long Beach Peninsula, 5 miles away as the gull flies but 90 miles by road.***

## TOKELAND

Set on the long peninsula reaching into northern Willapa Bay, this crabbing community, named after 19th-century Chief Toke, is the loneliest part of the southwest coast, where the omnipresent tackiness of contemporary resort life is least apparent. Just before you reach Tokeland Peninsula, you find a stretch of Highway 105 that's as unpeopled as one could wish, with turnouts for a restorative view of open ocean and breakers attacking the shore. Just beyond here the tiny Shoalwater Bay Indian Tribe has opened a modest casino, but the status quo hasn't changed much. In Tokeland, seize the day and pick up a container of crabmeat and some cocktail sauce from Nelson Crab (3088 Kindred Avenue; 360/267-2911), open daily from 9am to 5pm, to enjoy while sitting on a beach.

## LODGINGS

### TOKELAND HOTEL

Near the end of a sandy peninsula on the north shore of Willapa Bay, this great old place deserves high marks for longevity (at 104 years, it's the oldest resort hotel in the state) and for continuing to draw devotees of its easygoing hospitality. Scott and Catherine White wage a valiant battle to keep things up to snuff, and the results are heartening. All 18 rooms on the second floor have been completely redone; they're neat and well maintained, nicely furnished with period pieces, perhaps a bit Spartan but that doesn't mean the mattresses are lumpy. Baths are down the hall. Some rooms have views of pristine Willapa Bay. Guests find plenty of comfortable spots to relax, whether sunning in the meadow or on a driftwood log on the beach or reading in the fireplace room off the lobby. The restaurant does a creditable job, and is well patronized by locals who come to take advantage of hearty portions at reasonable prices. Expect down-home cooking and due deference to fresh local specialties like oysters, crab, and cranberries (perhaps cranberry sausage for breakfast, or cranberry pot roast for Sunday dinner). Breakfast, not included with the room, may offer eggs and hashbrowns or a generous hangtown fry.

Pets are not permitted. *100 Hotel Rd, Tokeland; Kindred Ave and Hotel Rd; 360/267-7006; $$; D, MC, V; local checks only; breakfast, lunch, and dinner every day; hotel and restaurant open weekends only, Dec to Feb; beer and wine.*

# SOUTH BEND

This picturesque but sleepy burg, county seat of Pacific County, is perched on the evergreen bluffs along the west shore of Willapa Bay, one of America's most pristine estuaries. Ruling over the town is the historic County Courthouse (at Memorial and Cowlitz), with its splendid art-glass dome. (It was denounced by some fiscal sourpusses as a "gilded palace of extravagance" when it opened in 1910.) South Bend bills itself as "Oyster Capital of the World." That's a classic bit of boosterism, but the Willapa Bay oysters are world-class. You can't miss the piles of oyster shells north of town and the "EZ-IN-EZ-OUT" invitations to buy. Also on Highway 101 just north of town, the H & H Cafe (360/875-5442) is still the place to stop for pie.

***Stop at the Pacific County Museum (1008 West Robert Bush Drive in South Bend) and get maps of self-guided tours of the historic homes on the hill, and of the courthouse with its colorful art-glass dome and murals of Willapa Bay history—painted by a jail inmate in the 1940s.***

## ACTIVITIES

SHOPS ***Sweater Heaven.*** Stop and snap up a colorful sweater and you'll be toasty-warm on mountain trails or breezy beaches. Willapa Bay Knits (302 Robert Bush Drive, South Bend; 360/875-6063), a cottage industry housed in South Bend's onetime opera house, offers a rainbow selection of generously cut unisex sweaters at incredibly good prices. They're all handloomed on the premises, of wools and silks from Italy, cottons, and various blends. For tips on how to care for your purchase, just ask Anni, who's always on hand.

## RESTAURANTS

### GARDNER'S ★★

After the courthouse, the next best roadside attraction in South Bend is Gardner's, where succulent baked oysters on the half shell and most everything else, from cheeseburgers to fettuccine, is prepared with wonderful attention to detail by chef/manager Gerry Schultz. Gerry makes everything from scratch, to order, and offers intriguing variations of basic standbys: halibut may be baked, poached, or grilled, each with its own distinctive sauce or seasoning. For halibut as it should be (moist and tender, not overcooked) try it simply poached, with a sprinkling of fresh dill, red onion, and capers. Gerry's homemade cheesecake gets high marks. The wine list, though not extensive, offers most of the best-known Northwest labels. Come for lunch and choose from a dozen and a half sandwiches, and many of the dinner salads and entrees. Or if you can't take time to sit down, a drive-through in front offers food to go—try the Caesar wrap (Caesar salad in a tortilla). *702 W Robert Bush Dr, South Bend; on Hwy 101; 360/875-5154; $$; AE, DC, DIS, MC, V; checks OK; lunch and dinner every day, breakfast on weekends; beer and wine.*

## RAYMOND

Raymond is a river town through and through, clinging to the lazy Willapa and remembering its boom times when it was one of the state's busiest shipping and logging centers. A new maritime museum preserves the memories, and nearby a paved riverside trail leads past a 100-foot sailing ship permanently anchored at the pier. A picturesque 3½-mile trail follows the river all the way to South Bend. Most motorists hurry through Raymond on their way to the beach. But Raymond has found a way to get even, practically forcing travelers to slow down and maybe even stop.

### ACTIVITIES

***The Sculpture Corridor.*** Along Highway 101 from one end to the other of "Raymond on the Willapa," as it has christened itself, and here and there throughout town and by the river, fantastically lifelike steel sculptures will have your eyes popping: an Indian fisherman landing a salmon, a gull on a post, a pair of loggers sawing a log in half, bears in the grass, a woman with a flower cart (with real flowers), a doe with her fawns—all looking as though arrested in motion. There are over 200 of these sculptures, thanks to the collaboration of the city and three southwest Washington artists, and the community's support. Photographers can't resist them, artists acclaim them, and children are enchanted by them.

# LONG BEACH PENINSULA

# LONG BEACH PENINSULA

Stretching its southern limits a bit, the Long Beach Peninsula could be said to extend from Chinook and Ilwaco on the Columbia River north to Leadbetter Point, which curves like a fishtail into the northern waters of Willapa Bay. This southernmost corner of Washington has attracted vacationers since the late 1900s, when fine lodgings, fresh oysters, and the broad beaches were the attractions. They still are, along with the beautiful Fort Canby and Leadbetter Point State Parks.

## CHINOOK

Nestled on the shores of Baker Bay—part of the broad Columbia River estuary—Chinook was formerly a profitable salmon fish-trapping center. The too-efficient fish traps were outlawed in 1935 and the wooden pilings in the bay, whose tops you can see at low tide, are all that remains of Chinook's heyday, when its harbor was a maze of pilings and nets and the town claimed the highest per capita income in the country. But Chinook is still a fish town, with a packing plant, a salmon hatchery, and 400 slips in the harbor.

### ACTIVITIES

***Fort Columbia State Park.*** Two miles southeast of Chinook on Highway 101 is a cluster of restored turn-of-the-century wooden buildings where soldiers were once stationed to guard the mouth of the Columbia River from foreign invasion. The former commander's house is now a military museum; huge cannons were once housed in the forbidding concrete bunkers. The gun emplacements have been restored and two coastal artillery guns have been brought from other forts. There is no camping but a youth hostel is nearby; 360/777-8755. The park claims some of the area's largest rhododendron bushes and superb views of the Columbia and the huge span of the Astoria-Megler Bridge. Climb steep Scarborough Hill behind the fort for the best view. Open daily, April through September, but hours vary; 360/777-8221 or 360/642-3078.

## RESTAURANTS

### THE SANCTUARY ☆

Chinook's old Methodist church couldn't have found a better second life: as a site for praiseworthy meals served by owner/chef Joanne Leech. Here, amid stained-glass windows, a pump organ, and cherubs, she offers an eclectic menu inspired by the Pacific Rim, by the local Scandinavian heritage, and by the plenitude of fresh local provender like shellfish, salmon, and woodland mushrooms. Try the *svenska kottbullar* (Swedish meatballs) and *fiskekaker* (Scandinavian fish cakes)—both of which can be sampled as appetizers. Innovative preparations might include fresh salmon with a crunchy potato crust, or a filet mignon served with a zingy Jack Daniel's mustard sauce. She also purveys the area's best home-baked bread. For dessert, homemade lemon cream sherbet is heavenly, ditto for the *krumkakke.* Lighter fare is served in the Library, an alcove where dinner music sometimes issues from the grand piano. *794 Hwy 101, Chinook; Hwy 101 at Hazel; 360/777-8380; $$; AE, MC, V; checks OK; dinner Wed–Sun (winter hours vary); full bar.* ♿

## ILWACO

***Lieutenant Charles Wilkes wrote of the Columbia Bar in 1841: "Mere description can give little idea of the terrors of the bar. All who have seen it have spoken of the wildness of the scene and the incessant roar of the waters . . . one of the most fearful sights that can possibly meet the eye."***

Today, Ilwaco is best known as a fishing center. But long before salmon was king, it was the transportation hub, by buggy, train, and boat, for the areas on both sides of the Columbia. Walk its downtown streets to see murals on fine old commercial buildings, faithfully depicting the town's past. In summer the colorful waterfront is as good as a circus. Vendors of souvenirs and snacks ply their wares, and charter companies vie for your business. Here where the Columbia River meets the Pacific, you're invited to head out for salmon, sturgeon, steelhead, and bottom fish. Charter fishing is open primarily May through October, with an occasional bottom-fishing excursion at other times. Some operators offer deep-sea tuna trips in summer. With salmon fishing so unpredictable now, many are offering whale-watching tours. Call ahead for season openings and reservations. You can get a list of the numerous charter companies from the Long Beach Peninsula Visitor's Bureau; 800/451-2542.

## ACTIVITIES

***Ilwaco Heritage Museum.*** There are enticements here for everyone: it's an art gallery, community center, and heritage museum, with information on Native Americans, explorers, fishermen, farmers, commercial cranberry growers, and, more recently, local kite flyers. An annex—a restoration of the old railroad depot—has an operating scale model of the "Clamshell Railway," which linked Ilwaco and the peninsula with steamers from Astoria, Oregon. Open daily in summer, Monday through Saturday in winter (115 SE Lake Street; 206/642-3446).

***There've been no trains in Ilwaco since 1930, but you can pretend: one of the town's murals shows a locomotive coming full-bore down the street, straight toward you.***

***Fort Canby State Park.*** In 1862, Fort Canby was established to protect the mouth of the Columbia. It's now the 1,800-acre Fort Canby State Park, the only state park on the Long Beach Peninsula allowing camping, with 250 sites. Not surprisingly, it fills up fast in summer. Call as far ahead as possible, since August sites are usually filled up by the end of the previous January, or reserve by mail beginning January 1 (PO Box 488, Ilwaco, WA 98624; 800/562-0900 or 360/642-3078). Your only chance of getting drop-in space in July or August is if there is a cancellation. The best tent sites are those closest to the ocean (91–110 or 161–180).

***A great place to chow is the Galley (133 Howerton Way, Ilwaco; 360/642-8700), a bright little spot of sunshine on the pier for fish and chips, or clam chowder served in a hollowed-out sourdough bread bowl.***

***Lewis and Clark Interpretive Center.*** Located in Fort Canby, this center dramatically details the expedition's travels with huge murals, paintings, photos, and excerpts from original journals. Your reward for going all the way with the captains is a breathtaking view of the ocean through huge windows in the last room. The world's only National Motor Life Boat School is located here, where the ocean's treacherous conditions allow coast guard personnel to practice in the 44-foot motor lifeboats virtually every day. The school offers no organized tours, but if you catch the watch-stander on a good day, you might get to stroll around those unsinkable boats; 360/642-3029.

***The Lights Still Shine.*** A trail from the Lewis and Clark Interpretive Center leads to the Cape Disappointment Lighthouse, while one from the Route 100 Loop (State Park Road) gets you to North Head Lighthouse. Both were built in the last century and are still operating, though only North Head has tours (in summer; $1 per head). Both also offer superlative views of the seductive beaches and the treacherous river mouth where so many ships have come to grief.

***Fisherman's Barbecue.*** For a fresh-air picnic, buy some fresh seafood at Jessie's Ilwaco Fish (West End and Port Docks; 360/642-3773), take it to the city park at the end of Lake Street on Baker Bay, and have yourself a fisherman's barbecue.

## RESTAURANTS

### BUBBA'S PIZZA

***Next best thing to living in a lighthouse: rent the Keeper's Residence at the North Head Lighthouse, which sleeps eight, for $200 a night. Call 360/642-3078.***

After a brief sojourn in Seaview, Bubba's is back where it belongs, on the Ilwaco waterfront. It's not much to look at, inside or out, but the aroma of fresh-baked pizza dough, garlic, provolone, and pepperoni will entice you through the door. Once inside, chef Bubba Kuhn's artistry, wit, and showmanship (every pie is hand-tossed, and Kuhn keeps up a running commentary throughout) will keep you entertained. All the usuals are here, plus the Man Overboard (10 toppings); the Farm (olive oil instead of sauce, with garlic, herbs, and a ton of veggies); and the Land Lubber (shrimp, oysters, mushrooms, olives, and tomatoes). You can get a Greek salad with real Greek olives, and a shrimp salad with half a pound of shrimp. Watch the show while your pizza is being tossed, then eat it with a glass of Chianti at a window table, with a view of the sun setting over hundreds of boats. *177 SE Howerton Way, Ilwaco; on the waterfront at SE Howerton; 360/642-8700; www.bubbaspizza.com; $; MC, V; checks OK; dinner Wed–Sun; beer and wine.* ♿

## LODGINGS

### THE INN AT ILWACO ★

In a quiet cul-de-sac overlooking the town, this shingled, steepled bed-and-breakfast has preserved a good measure of serenity from the years when it was Ilwaco's Presbyterian church. Under new owners Ed and Karen Bussone the chapel, recently a breakfast room, has regained its former dignity. The gift shop is gone from the vestibule and the pews are back in the sanctuary, where concerts are sometimes held. Once the parish hall, the parlor–sitting room, with its fireplace and comfortable chairs doubles as breakfast room. Six guest rooms are tucked into dormers and under the eaves on the second floor; three more are on the main floor, including a suite that sleeps four and has a fireplace and fridge. All rooms have private baths. *120 Williams St NE, PO Box 922, Ilwaco; off 4th to end of Williams St; 888/244-2523 or 360/642-8686; bussone@longbeachlodging.com; www.longbeachlodging.com; $$–$$$; MC, V; checks OK.*

### CHINA BEACH BED & BREAKFAST RETREAT ★★

Another gem from David Campiche and Laurie Anderson of the Shelburne Inn, this secluded hideaway on Baker Bay offers privacy, repose, and every creature comfort. The 1907 house has been transformed into a three-bedroom inn, beautifully furnished with antiques and with the spotting scope in place at the picture window, in case a heron or eagle comes in view. No TV—but the ebb and flow of the tide, the birds on the beach, and the spectacular sunsets are show enough. Have a beach fire, borrow the kayak, doze on the deck. A continental breakfast may be taken here, or guests may opt for the full-scale production at the Shelburne Inn, two minutes away. No pets. *222 Robert Gray Drive, Ilwaco; PO Box 250, Seaview; get directions at the Shelburne when you check in; 360/642-5660 or 360/642-2442; innkeeper@theshelburneinn.com; www.chinabeachretreat.com; $$$; AE, MC, V; checks OK.*

## SEAVIEW

Seaview is the first town on the Long Beach Peninsula, the slender finger of land dividing Willapa Bay from the Pacific. With Highway 103 as its backbone, the peninsula is famous for its 37-mile-long flat stretch of public beach (reputedly the longest such stretch worldwide); its gentle marine climate; its exhibition kite flying; its cranberry bogs, clamming, and rhododendrons; and its food, which is unequaled by any like-size area on the Northwest Coast. Some of the Long Beach Peninsula's prettiest stretches (and a couple of its finest restaurants and lodgings) are tucked into this small beachfront community at the peninsula's southern end. Almost every westward road leads to the beach, where you can park your car, stroll the quaint neighborhoods, and traverse the rolling dunes.

## ACTIVITIES

***Art for Sale.*** The Charles Mulvey Gallery displays the quintessential peninsula watercolors of ocean, beach, and bay; 46th Place & L St; 360/642-2189.

***Ancient Cedars.*** Accessible only by your own boat, Long Island at the lower end of Willapa Bay harbors an ancient self-perpetuating cedar grove, with some trees over 200 feet tall and 1,000 years old. Walk along the road from the boat landing for 2½ miles, and take the loop trail. The island is part of the Willapa Bay National Wildlife Refuge, with headquarters on Highway 101, back on the mainland and 10 miles north of Seaview; 360/484-3482. If you row or paddle to the island, check tides; currents are strong in the narrow channel, and at low tide the bottom is very close.

## RESTAURANTS

### 42ND STREET CAFE ★★

Cheri and Blaine Walker know how to keep the customers coming back to this popular spot just down the highway from the Shelburne Inn. American fare shares the spotlight with a more imaginative menu of pasta and unusual sauces (port wine and cranberry, for one). You can count on comfy-cozy decor, cheerful waitresses, and hearty portions of home cooking (berry conserves and corn relish, iron-skillet-fried chicken). Local oysters are featured in a number of creations, and desserts are terrific. Good news: Now you may come for breakfast too. *4201 Pacific Hwy, Seaview; corner of 42nd St; 360/642-2323; the42ndstcafe@hotmail.com; $$; DIS, MC, V; checks OK; breakfast, lunch, and dinner every day; beer and wine.* ♿

### THE HERON AND BEAVER PUB ★★

While the adjoining and much more formal Shoalwater gets all the acclaim (same owners, same kitchen, a great deal of menu overlap), the Heron and Beaver remains a pint-size destination in its own right. In this cozy, crowded slip of a bar you might slurp down Willapa Bay oyster shooters doused with a vodka-and-pepper-kicking cocktail sauce, and chased with a microbrew. Indulge in spicy blackened oysters or an Asian-inspired Dungeness crab cake. Or go for a BLT with Canadian bacon and basil-pesto mayo, or a burger anointed with homemade cranberry-blueberry mustard. Explore the extensive wine menu, sample single-malt Scotches. *4415 Pacific Hwy, Seaview; in the Shelburne Inn, Pacific Hwy 103 and N 45th; 360/642-4142; $$; AE, DC, MC, V; checks OK; lunch Mon–Sat, dinner every day, brunch Sun; full bar.* ♿

### MY MOM'S PIE KITCHEN & CHOWDER HOUSE

Donna Wilkie has moved the restaurant of her longtime friend, the late Jeanne McLaughlin, a mile down the road, and the name still says it all: this small establishment serves a host of irresistible homemade pies and other luscious concoctions. Pies include banana cream, pecan, sour cream–raisin, rhubarb, and more, depending on the time of year and, in some cases, the time of day. Arrive too late (especially in summer), and this sweetnik's haven might be sold out of your favorite (good excuse to try a new variety). Before savoring a slice, have a steamy bowl of chowder (probably the peninsula's best) or a crab quiche. Eat inside, where it's as cheery and dainty as your grandmom's summer parlor, or on the porch. *4316 W Pacific Hwy, Seaview; Pacific Hwy and Seaview; 360/642-2342; $; no credit cards; checks OK; lunch Wed–Sun; no alcohol.*

### THE SHOALWATER (THE SHELBURNE INN) ★★★

Longtime owners Ann and Tony Kischner's devotion to fine foodstuffs and fabulous wine continues to make the Shoalwater the Northwest's most beloved destination dining spot. The elegant main salon, with its tongue-and-groove walls and ceiling, brass light fixtures, fine watercolors, and grandfather clock, resembles a first-class captain's cabin. Back in the kitchen, chef Lynne Pelletier takes the helm, offering native ingredients that bow to the season. Willapa Bay oysters (none fresher), wild mushrooms (Long Beach is a forager's dream), and salal berries (flavoring a vinaigrette that may be bought by the bottle) highlight a seafood-heavy menu that pays due homage to meat and chicken. Those with a sweet tooth can thank pastry chef Ann Kischner, whose professional hand with desserts deserves applause. *4415 Pacific Hwy, Seaview; Pacific Hwy 103 and N 45th; 360/642-4142; wine&dine@willapabay.org; www.shoalwater.com; $$$; AE, DC, DIS, MC, V; checks OK; lunch, dinner every day; full bar.* ♿

## LODGINGS

### THE SHELBURNE INN ★★★

The last stronghold of dignity before the hubbub of Long Beach up the road, the century-old Shelburne Inn combines its appeal to hedonists with a great location—just a few quiet blocks from the ocean. All rooms are bright, cheerful, and immaculate, furnished with choice antiques and private baths and cozy homespun quilts on queen-size beds. South-facing rooms have private decks or balconies. Don't expect the modern amenities (sauna, Jacuzzis) that have become de rigueur at so many chic hideaways. The third-floor rooms are the best buys; they still have gently slanting floors (the entire building was pulled across the street by a team of horses in 1911). But squeakfree flooring and carpeting have been installed throughout. Breakfasts—they're included in the rates—are superb, served at a big table in the lobby that almost groans under the feast. Innkeepers David Campiche and Laurie Anderson whip up satisfying eye-openers of razor-clam cakes or scrambled eggs with smoked salmon, chives (from the inn's herb garden), and Gruyère cheese—not to mention the pastries. The separately owned Shoalwater (see review) is the dinner restaurant. *PO Box 250, Seaview; Pacific Hwy 103 and N 45th; 800/INN-1896 or 360/642-2441; innkeeper@the shelburneinn.com; www.the shelburneinn.com; $$$; AE, MC, V; checks OK.* ♿

### SOU'WESTER LODGE ★

This place is definitely not for everyone, but those who appreciate good conversation, a sense of humor, and rambling lodgings on the beach will find Leonard and Miriam Atkins's humble, old-fashioned resort just what the doctor ordered. The main structure was built in 1892 as a summer home for U.S. Senator Henry Winslow Corbett, and now offers a variety of rooms and apartments. You can also stay in fully equipped cabins or a collection of classic trailers—"Spartan accommodations for the impecunious," Leonard says. The hosts are as much a draw as the lodgings. Originally from South Africa, they came to Long Beach in 1980 by way of Israel and Chicago. The view from the lodge's balcony—across windswept, grassy dunes to the sea—is enough to keep anyone here permanently. Books, periodicals, videos, and CDs almost overwhelm the living room, which occasionally hosts lectures, chamber music concerts, painting workshops, and theatricals. Leonard has dubbed the joint the official outpost of the "B&(MYOD)B" club—Bed and (Make Your Own Damn) Breakfast. New attraction, thanks to a guest who is an enthusiastic gardener: masses of flowers around the inn and a meditation garden. *PO Box 102, Seaview; 1½ blocks southwest of Seaview's traffic light on Beach Access Rd (38th Pl); 360/642-2542; $; MC, V; checks OK.*

***"Life is desperate here but never serious."—Leonard Atkins of the Sou'wester Lodge***

## LONG BEACH

The major town on the Long Beach Peninsula, Long Beach is full of commotion in the summer, and relatively calm and collected the rest of the year. But it's summer when the festivals happen and the sun shines warmly, so don't stay away, but do plan ahead. Even though bed and breakfasts and motels are multiplying, reservations are always a good idea. So is visiting during spring, when the tides are low enough in the daytime for clam digging, or early fall, when the salmon—and charter companies—are still running.

***Long Beach's new 2-mile-long Dune Trail stretches from 17th Street S to 16th Street NW and welcomes walkers, bikers, and runners—no motorized contraptions.***

To get a feel for Long Beach, make for the half-mile-long elevated boardwalk (with night lighting) stretching between S 10th and Bolstad Streets, accessible by wheelchairs, baby strollers,

*You want mobility? Rent a Honda moped or a three-wheeled bike for fun on the beach at O.W.W. Inc., at the 10th Street approach to the beach, near the Go-Kart track; 360/642-4260.*

bicycles, and good old footpower. Along the way there are interpretive signs, to help you understand this land of dunes and sea. Then head for the beach. The great thing about this stretch of hard, flat sand is that you can do practically anything you like. You can walk, run, sit, fly kites, dig clams, ride horses or mountain bikes, sculpt a sand castle, and even drive your car. There are some limitations on beach driving; check with the Visitors Bureau. If you plan to dig razor clams, call the Department of Fisheries in Nahcotta for information; 360/249-4628.

## ACTIVITIES

***Festival Fun.*** This place is festival-happy and no wonder, with all that beach to spread out on. Memorial Day weekend sees the World's Longest Garage Sale. Come in June for the World's Longest Beach Run and the Northwest Garlic Festival, an event which must be seen, tasted, and sniffed to be believed. July's SandSations, a sand-sculpting contest, attracts artists and gawkers from near and far. The Visitors Bureau, 800/451-2542, will tell you more.

***A Helping Hand.*** The extraordinarily helpful Long Beach Peninsula Visitors Bureau will help you find your heart's desire on the peninsula, with lists of lodgings, information on festivals, and advice on charter fishing, among other diversions. At the junction of Highways 101 and 103 (PO Box 562, Long Beach; 800/451-2542 or 360/642-2400; www.funbeach.com.

***Flying High.*** The constant coastal winds make kite flying a passion; Long Beach boasts three kite shops. The oldest is Stormin' Norman (205 S Pacific Highway; 360/642-3482), which hides at the back of the shop a huge stock of reasonably priced kites. Ocean Kites (511 Pacific Highway; 800/KITE-FLY or 360/642-2229) has been voted America's best kite shop. Long Beach Kites (104 Pacific Highway; 360/642-2202) stocks kites from all over the world and sells numerous hard-to-find parts.

*The Dragon's Den at the Kite Museum in Long Beach displays huge, fearsome dragon kites from the Orient—including one that's more than 200 feet long.*

***A World of Kites.*** Drop in at the World Kite Museum (N 3rd Street and Pacific Highway; 360/642-4020) to see displays of Asian fighter kites, locally made flyers, ancient kites, and exotic, shimmering flying art. $4 for families, $1.50 for adults, and $1 for kids and seniors; open only on weekends unless you call ahead.

***International Kite Festival.*** Held in mid-August, this annual event brings thousands of soaring creations to the skies, and the beach looks like three county fairs in one. There are contests for most kites in the air, aerial ballet, best home-made kite, highest kite—the sky's the limit. There's even a mobile kite hospital for emergency repairs. It's fun, but don't wait until the last minute to reserve lodgings.

***Saddle Up.*** Horseback riding on the beach is the stuff of dreams. An hour ($11) at Skip Kotek's Skipper's Equestrian Center (9th Street S and Beach Blvd; 360/642-3676) gets you a 5-mile beach ride. Bring your own horse and for a small fee you (and your critter) can set up camp at Long Beach's rodeo ground; or rent a stall at Skip Kotek's spread, out in the country.

***Sweet and Hot.*** Milton York Candy Company, on the main drag (109 Pacific Highway S; 360/642-2352), has been here since 1892 producing candy from founder York's original recipes. Besides luscious chocolates and ice cream, come for breakfast, lunch, and dinner. Across the street, the Cottage Bakery (118 Pacific Highway S) does a land-office business in pies, sweet stuff, cakes, and rolls, and also serves espresso, soups, and sandwiches. For spicy-hot Mexican, head for Las Maracas (515 Pacific Highway S; 360/642-8000).

***Art with a Park.*** Campiche Studios, at the corner of 5th and Pacific Highway S (504 Pacific Highway S; 360/642-4142) has lovely art glass; watercolors; unusual pottery including works by Nancy Campiche's brother David, of Shelburne Inn fame; and a little courtyard on the street, with benches and a pool where a striking rock-sculpture fountain makes soothing music.

***Six and a half miles north of Long Beach, on Sandridge Road, Clarke's Nursery grows fields of rhododendrons in 1,000 varieties, an exhilarating springtime display. Open daily in summer, weekdays in winter; 360/ 642-2241.***

## RESTAURANTS

### MAX'S ★

This diminutive, elongated eatery purveys upward of 100 menu choices: appetizers such as fried artichoke hearts wrapped with bacon and escargots baked in a mornay sauce; elegant seafood entrees including cashew prawns and salmon stuffed with cream cheese. Steamed clams, mussels, and grilled steaks are on offer, in various fashions. Service is beachtown friendly. *111 S Pacific Hwy, Long Beach; 360/642-5600; $$; AE, DIS, MC, V; no checks; lunch and dinner every day; full bar.*

## LODGINGS

### BOREAS BED & BREAKFAST ★

Boreas is a picturesque lodging in a postcard-perfect setting rampant with flower beds. A remodeled 1920s beach house, it's tastefully decorated with antiques and contemporary art, and appointed with handsome furnishings. Owners Susie Goldsmith and Bill Verner have created five sumptuous suites, all with private baths (one with jetted tub) and varying views of dunes, ocean, and gardens. There's a hot tub inside a glassed-in sundeck for year-round soaking and a backyard deck that's private and out of the wind. The beach is a short walk through the dunes. *607 N Boulevard, PO Box 1344, Long Beach; on N Boulevard, 1 block west of the main drag; 888/642-8069; 360/642-8069; boreas@boreasinn.com; www.boreasinn.com; $$; AE, DC, DIS, MC, V; checks OK.*

# OCEAN PARK

Ocean Park, founded as a religious settlement more than a century ago, is now a tranquil retirement community set along the beach, with new condominiums sharing the town with idiosyncratic old houses that were built with salvaged logs and lumber. The beach is quiet except in June, when the Garlic Festival takes over the town; call the Ocean Park Chamber of Commerce, 800/451-2542, for the date as well as other community information.

## ACTIVITIES

***Galleries.*** The Wiegardt Studio Gallery (2607 Bay Avenue; 360/665-5976) displays Eric Wiegardt seascapes in a restored Victorian house. Nearby, the Shoalwater Cove Galleries exhibit Marie Powell's nature scenes, done in soft pastels

(25612 Sandridge Road; 360/665-6955; shoalwatr@aone.com; www.aone.com/~shoalwtr).

***Specialty Foods.*** At P&K Seafood Market, a little clapboard house, shop for packed and smoked fish, huckleberry syrup, and local jams. You can take your shrimp cocktail and clam chowder out to a picnic table by the shop for instant gratification (25312 Highway 103; Pacific Highway and 254th Place; 800/519-3518 or 360/665-6800).

## LODGINGS

### BLACKWOOD BEACH COTTAGES ★

Five dusky-red cottages face the grassy dunes and the sea. Four more hide behind them in the pines. These are Blackwood Beach Cottages, which look as though they'd been there for years—as much a part of the landscape as the driftwood and gulls. But they're less than three years old, as you'll see when you enter the spanking bright, elegantly furnished interiors. Peggy and Jim Bleckov (he was a builder by trade) saw the possibilities of this slice of seashore in Ocean Park and made it into a choice little resort: cutting as few trees as possible, encouraging native shrubbery, and siting the cottages for maximum view or privacy or both. All but one of the cottages are one-bedroom and have kitchens; the exception contains two separate units identical to the others except for no kitchens. The beach, only a few steps away, is far less populated than teeming Long Beach to the south, yet every bit as wide and sandy, and it catches the same gusty winds to keep your kite swooping through the air. Peggy urges you to visit the thriving herb and vegetable garden and help yourself. Labels list reputed benefits. When you learn that artichokes are conducive to romance, it could change your mind about the dinner menu. The Bleckovs are zealous about keeping their guests warm. The electric heat instantly springs to life, most units have gas fireplaces, and Peggy, a bedding maven, provides feather beds, down comforters, and mountains of feather and down pillows. When the sun sets or the weather takes a turn, snuggle in front of the fire, open a bottle of wine (there's more in the office shop if you run out), pop a movie in the VCR, and let the winds blow. One cottage is wheelchair-accessible. *20711 Pacific Hwy, Ocean Park; 8 miles north of Seaview, 2 miles south of Ocean Beach; 888/376-6356 or 360/665-6356; www.willapabay.org/~opchamber/blackwood; $$$; DIS, MC V; checks OK.*

### KLIPSAN BEACH COTTAGES ☆

A row of eight small, separate, well-maintained older cottages stands facing the ocean in a parklike setting of pine trees and clipped lawns. Since these are individually owned condominiums, interior decoration schemes can vary widely, but all of the immaculate units feature fireplaces (or woodstoves), full kitchens, TVs, and ocean-facing decks just a couple of hundred feet from the beach. A pleasant gazebo has barbecue equipment. Children are fine, but no pets. It's a peaceful place, fully booked all summer. *22617 Pacific Hwy, Ocean Park; Hwy 103, 2 miles south of Ocean Park; 360/665-4888; klipsanbeachcottages.com; www.klipsanbeachcottages.com; $$–$$$; MC, V; checks OK.* ♿

### SHAKTI COVE COTTAGES ☆

Ten little cabins on 3 forested acres within earshot of the thundering Pacific cater to happy campers looking for a home-away-from-home at the beach. Covekeepers Celia and Liz Cavalli's welcome extends to guests with pets, even large canines, and to the cottages' loyal gay and lesbian clientele (homophobes will be more comfortable elsewhere). The rustic but spotlessly clean cottages have complete kitchens, cable TV, no phones, and private carports, to say nothing of easy access to a stunning stretch of beach. Jack's Country Store (if they don't have it, you don't need it) is a short walk away at Pacific Highway and Bay Avenue, in case you forgot to bring soap or soup. *PO Box 385, Ocean Park; on 253rd Pl (1 block west of Pacific Hwy 103); 360/665-4000; $$; MC, V; checks OK.*

## NAHCOTTA

Nahcotta has become almost synonymous with oysters. At the Nahcotta Oyster Farm (270th and Sandridge Road, on the old rail line), you can pick up some pesticide-free oysters or gather your own for half-price. Jolly Roger Seafoods (across from The Ark, 360/665-4111) is also a good bet. The Nahcotta Natural Store (270th and Sandridge Road, 360/665-4449) is a pleasant stop for beverages and grub.

## RESTAURANTS

### THE ARK ★★

The Ark, which sits among the canneries and the mountains of oyster shells at the old Nahcotta dock, has become a legend, thanks to accolades from the likes of the late James Beard. It's hard to live up to such a reputation decade after decade, but on the whole the restaurant still pleases. You can't get seafood much fresher, and when oysters on the half shell are on the menu (in season), you're looking out at the very beds where they were reared. The Ark oyster feed (the record is 110) of Willapa Bay bivalves, lightly breaded and pan-fried, still excels. Whatever you do, try not to fill up on the great herb-spiced rolls while you wait for your appetizer—perhaps Asian-style grilled eggplant, or a duo of scampi kindly sautéed with tomatoes, mushrooms, and onions. Willapa Bay sturgeon with mushrooms, sun-dried tomatoes, and balsamic vinegar is a wise choice. Or go for a lighter and less pretentious menu in the Willapa Room, as the pub is now known; it has its own entrance so you need not force your way through the sometimes crowded chattery dining room. If linguini graced with prawns, tomatoes, garlic, Parmesan, and hazelnuts is on the menu, lucky you. The ratatouille, served with polenta and goat cheese, garnished with basil or rosemary, could have come straight from the Mediterranean. *273rd and Sandridge Rd, Nahcotta; on the old Nahcotta dock, next to the oyster fleet; 360/665-4133; $$$; AE, DC, DIS, MC, V; dinner Tues–Sun (Thurs–Sun in winter); brunch Sun; full bar.*

***Improve your oyster knowledge: visit the Willapa Field Station (267 Sandridge Road; 360/665-4166), which has outdoor interpretive signs, maps, and info; while Willapa Bay Interpretive Center (on the Nahcotta pier near the Ark, open summer weekends only) features a viewing deck and indoor exhibits.***

*Recommended reading before you visit Oysterville:* **Oysterville: Roads to Grandpa's Village**, *a loving, funny memoir by the late Willard Espy. The Espy house, oldest in town (1863) is just south of the church.*

## LODGINGS

### MOBY DICK HOTEL & OYSTER FARM ☆

Although it looks fairly institutional at first glance, this friendly place grows on you. The hotel, originally built in 1929 by a railroad conductor with his gold-prospecting money, is under the careful ownership of Fritzie and Edward Cohen (of the Tabard Inn in Washington, D.C.). It's quite beachy (without really having a beach), with a couple of spacious public rooms, eight small and modest bedrooms (most with shared bath), and a rambling bay front (loaded with oysters). In the afternoon, join the innkeepers for a few Pacific oysters on the half shell. A very private sauna is tucked away in a cedar grove overlooking the bay. Full breakfasts (included) make use of the hotel's own garden produce. As in virtually every other place in Nahcotta, you can buy oysters here too. Pets welcome. Dinners are offered (for guests and others) off and on, depending on whether the chef is in residence. Call ahead. *PO Box 82, Nahcotta; south of Bay Ave on Sandridge Rd; 360/665-4543; mobydickhotel@willapabay.org; $$; AE, MC, V; checks OK.*

*The snowy plover, a rare and threatened species, flies all the way from Mexico to nest on the Leadbetter Point beach, and the upper ocean beach is posted as closed, April to August. But there's plenty more beach for you to walk, and with binoculars and from a respectful distance, you might spy a plover that didn't read the signs.*

# OYSTERVILLE

Oysterville dates to 1854 and was the county seat until (legend has it) a group from South Bend stole the county records in 1893 because they didn't like having to travel so far for every little thing. South Bend remains the county seat to this day, but Oysterville (follow Sandridge Road north to the Oysterville sign) is a picturesque pocket of the past. It's listed on the National Register of Historic Places and features a double row of distinctive gingerbread-style homes, surrounded by stately cedars and spruce. There are no shops or services except a small store and the post office at the north end of town. But you may buy bivalves. Oysterville Sea Farms, at the old cannery in Oysterville, sells them by the dozen (open weekends, year-round).

## ACTIVITIES

***Leadbetter Point State Park.*** Leadbetter, on the northern tip of the peninsula, is part of the Willapa Bay National

Wildlife Refuge. Travel 3 miles north of Oysterville on Oysterville Road, then take Stackpole Road to the refuge. The park draws nature lovers year-round, with miles of trails—sandy in summer, muddy or even flooded in wet weather, when you may have to stick to the beach. More than 100 species of birds hang out here, and bird-watching is best during spring and fall migrations.

# HOOD CANAL

# HOOD CANAL

This narrow fjord stretches about 60 miles southwesterly from Admiralty Inlet, then changes its mind and swerves northeast for 25 miles, to peter out at Belfair. The peninsula within the "hook"—Tahuya Peninsula—is seeing more and more home-building along the shore, and there are several fine beach parks. But the interior is still largely undeveloped, especially at the southern end of the peninsula, mostly Tahuya State Forest and Department of Natural Resources lands. Northeast of Union, the short arm of Hood Canal is almost solid with mansions and modest homes, built over the decades by urbanites drawn by views of the Olympics and by the calm, swimmable waters. The western shore of the canal's long arm, where Highway 101 hugs the littoral, has stretches of forest and accessible beach. Three wild rivers plunge down from the Olympic Mountains to sedately enter the canal: the Duckabush, the Hamma Hamma, and the Dosewallips.

## SHELTON

Gateway to Hood Canal, Shelton is generally regarded as a timber town where sturdy loggers in cleated boots clomp about; as the center of an area that ships 2 million Christmas trees a year; and as a place where they take oyster-shucking deadly seriously. That's all pretty true, though the loggers may wear Nikes when they come to town these days. But timber is still very much a presence, and the Chamber of Commerce's Tourist Information Center is a 1907 Simpson Timber Co. caboose parked on a section of the old logging railroad track that runs through town.

### ACTIVITIES

***All About Mason County.*** If you can't make it to the caboose to find our more about Madison County, call the Chamber of Commerce at 800/576-2021 or 360/426-2021; e-mail coc@westsound.com; or visit their web page at www.westsound.com/coc.

***Aw, Shucks.*** Shelton's big event of the year is the Oysterfest and Seafood Festival, on the first weekend in October.

***The last working logging railroad in the Lower 48 is the Simpson Timber Co. road, a 40-mile track from Shelton to eastern Grays Harbor County.***

Shuckers vie for the West Coast Oyster Shucking Championship—the current record-holder shucked 24 oysters in 2 minutes and 44 seconds. It's a rousing small-town revel, with seafood specialties to sample, wine and microbrew tastings, touch tanks where you can get acquainted with sea creatures, and an oyster cook-off. Admission is $3 for adults, $2 for children and seniors, and a whole family can get in for $8. 360/426-2021.

***Hood Canal from On High.*** Olympic Air, at Sanderson Field in Shelton (N 11771 Highway 101; 360/426-1477), will take you flight-seeing over the canal or farther—maybe Mount St. Helens. The more daring can go skydiving with Blue Sky Skydiving Adventures, also at Sanderson Field; 800/801-JUMP.

***Tour the Forest.*** Simpson Timber Co. will take you on a timberland tour on summer Fridays to show you what's going on in their woods, and give you lunch. Tours are limited to ten people; children must be over 13; 360/427-4749.

***Prepare for a Plunge.*** Planning to see the canal below the surface? Divers will find everything they need at Mike's Diving Center, located at N 22270 Highway 101, Shelton, WA 98584; 360/877-9568.

***Prime Rib at the Park.*** Lake Nahwatzal Resort, 12 miles west of Shelton (W 12900 Shelton-Matlock Road; 360/426-8323) serves a popular prime rib dinner on Friday and Saturday nights. The restaurant is open every day. Have a meal or a drink on the deck with its lakeside view, or get into the swim—go water skiing, fishing, or sailing. The resort has cabins and RV hookups.

## RESTAURANTS

### STEVEN'S ☆

A bit over a year ago Steve and Angela Olson opened Steven's in downtown Shelton; Sheltonites are literally eating it up, and the word is getting out. The milieu is pretty enough for a Jane Austen novel, with a rich cranberry and blue decor and handsome antiques. Chef Steve does very well by seafood. He's rightly proud of his oysters, which he flours lightly, sautées, then tops them with a lemony meuniére

## SAMPLE THE SEAFOOD

***Here's a short list of places to find fresh local seafood, without getting your feet wet:***

***Hoodsport Inn, N 25141 Highway 101, Hoodsport; 360/877-6720; Hama Hama oysters grilled, fried, or in stew.***

***Hoodsport Marina and Cafe, N 24080 Highway 101; 360/877-9657; lightly sautéed oysters, homemade chowder, and razor clams.***

***Joan's, N 20031 Highway 101, Shelton; 360/877-6737; alder-smoked oysters, Native American smoked salmon.***

***Legends Restaurant, Little Creek Casino, Interchange Highway 101–108, Shelton; 360/427-7711; Thursday night seafood buffet, featuring local oysters.***

sauce enlivened with garlic and chives. Another winner is the royally rich crab-stuffed salmon with béchamel sauce. Even if you've no time for a meal, stop for a latte served in a stylish footed glass cup; take five on the big plump sofa in the entry; enjoy the flowery, civilized ambience while the ceiling fan turns overhead. *Steven's, 203 W Railroad Ave, Shelton; corner of 2nd and Railroad Ave; 360/426-4407; $$; MC, V; checks OK; lunch and dinner Tues-Sat; full bar; steven@hctc.com.* ♿

### XINH'S CLAM & OYSTER HOUSE ★★

Chef Xinh Dwelley knows her oysters. She's been quality control manager at Taylor United Inc., the Shelton shellfish company, for years. Today, with the backing of Taylor United, she runs not only Shelton's finest seafood restaurant, but one of the best (and freshest) little clam and oyster houses on the peninsula. Xinh herself picks out the best of each day's haul. Slide down a few Olympias or Steamboat Island Pacifics on the half shell and then see what Xinh can do with a sauce. You'll not find a better heaping plate of mussel meats in a Vietnamese curry sauce anywhere else. *221 W Railroad Ave, Shelton; at 3rd St and Railroad Ave; 360/427-8709; $$; MC, V; checks OK; dinner Tues–Sat; beer and wine.* ♿

***That mossy old waterwheel by the road near Union is the Dalby Waterwheel, built in 1922 and still working. Stop and snap a picture—everybody else does.***

# UNION AND THE EASTERN ARM

At the bottom of Hood Canal's "hook" you can travel north toward Port Townsend along the canal's main (western) arm, following Highway 101, or head for tiny Union and take Highway 106 along the short arm to Belfair. The views of the Olympics along this stretch are as spectacular as they get.

## ACTIVITIES

***Hunter Farms Market.*** Now that the fabulous Union Country Store is no more, Hunter Farms seems to be trying to fill the gap. Besides the expected country store basics, you'll find a few nice surprises, such as pint jars of apple or cherry cobbler at $4.95. They make scrumptious desserts, heated and served with cream or ice cream. During the growing season the store overflows with fruits and vegetables, inside and out. In season, shellfish from the canal are available. If you can't wait to open that oyster, get out your knife, find a table amid the piles of pumpkins and corn, and have at it. The store, on the left as you approach Union, is open all year (E 1921 Highway 106, Union; 360/898-2222 or 360/426-2222).

***Twanoh State Park.*** Popular with families with tots, Twanoh State Park provides access to the canal off Highway 106, 8 miles southwest of Belfair. Huge firs shade the grounds. There is a big, safe, shallow pool and a fast-food concession.

***Alderbrook Resort.*** Sprawling along the shore northeast of Union, Alderbrook has everything except the repose and quiet it offered before it grew into a highly touted conference center: golf course, marina, restaurant, view rooms, fitness centers, live entertainment (E 7101 Highway 106, Union, WA 98593; 800/622-9370).

***Hood Canal/Theler Wetlands.*** A mile and a half before you reach Belfair, stop at the Mary E. Theler Community Center, pick up a free guide, and explore a loop trail to freshwater and saltwater marshes, forested uplands, and the estuary where the Union River flows into Hood Canal. The 3.8-mile loop trail is wide and wheelchair-accessible. See birds, plant life, and beguiling views of Hood Canal. You'll come out with a lot more respect for wetlands—and with dry feet (E 22871 Highway 3, PO Box 1445, Belfair; 360/275-4898).

## RESTAURANTS

### VICTORIA'S

★★

This inviting stone and log structure on the east bank of Hood Canal has been a stopover spot since the early 1930s. Locals remember it as a lively dance hall and tavern, but in the last decade or so it has evolved into one of the better eateries on the canal. High-beamed ceilings, a fireplace, and large windows that look out on a nearby brook and sheltering trees set the scene for equally appealing food. Or you may eat out on the lawn or patio. The seafood can be exceptional, such as a generous bucket of Penn Cove mussels steamed in white wine and garlic. Portions of prime rib are ample, too. Desserts are imaginative—and rich. *E 6791 Hwy 106, Union; 1 mile west of Alderbrook Resort on Hwy 106; 360/898-4400; $$; MC, V; checks OK; lunch, dinner every day, breakfast Sun; full bar.* ♿

## LODGINGS

### ROBIN HOOD VILLAGE

This modest, low-key quasi-resort is a refreshing alternative to the only other lodgings along this stretch of Hood Canal, the overwhelming Alderbrook Resort. A private beach across the highway gives guests a place to enjoy the mountain view, take a dip, or launch a boat. The four chalet-style cottages have full kitchens, cable TV, and hot tubs; three have fireplaces. The smallest sleeps two, the largest ten. Behind the cottages, the "village" offers a liquor store, a hairdressing salon, a sauna, massage therapy, a launderette, and a gazebo for barbecues. On the other side of the driveway is Victoria's (see review, above); drop over for lunch or dinner. If you prefer a cozy meal by your own fireside, Victoria's will deliver. Or pick up provisions at Hunter Farms in Union and have a cook-in. Why not settle in for a week? Many do (and get a reduction in the rate). Pets are permit-

*At the Old Cedar Forge in Grapeview (east of Highway 3, the Shelton-Belfair Road), Jerry Culberson teaches the basics of blacksmithing, and doesn't mind if you visit his showroom and studio and watch him hammer away. You might find a candlestick or dinner bell you can't live without. 220 Cronquist Road, Grapeview; call 360/275-6769 for directions and hours.*

ted. *Robin Hood Village, 6780 E Hwy 106, Union; 1 mile west of Alderbrook Resort on Hwy 106; 360/898-2163; $$; DIS, MC, V; checks OK; robnhood@hctc.com.*

## BELFAIR

The town of Belfair, off Highway 3 at the canal's northeast tip, is a handy place to stock up for a picnic or a camping trip. From here, take the North Shore Road to such destinations on the Tahuya Peninsula as Tahuya and Belfair State Parks. Farther north (but more accessible by driving west from Bremerton), are tiny Seabeck and Scenic Beach State Park; see Kitsap Peninsula chapter.

## ACTIVITIES

**Parks and Adventures.** Of the parks along Hood Canal's eastern arm, Belfair State Park is the busiest. Located 3 miles southwest of Belfair on Highway 300 (North Shore Road), it's a place for families to swim, fish, fly kites, watch birds, and dig clams. Campers must reserve in summer; 800/452-5687. Farther south, overlooking the canal's big bend, are sprawling Tahuya State Park and Tahuya State Forest, reached from Belfair via the Belfair-Tahuya Road or Highway 300. The mostly wild park embraces beach and forest. Go mountain biking, hiking, or horseback riding. The Tahuya State Forest (largely second- or third-growth) is crisscrossed by multiple-use trails—that is, it's open to ORVers and motorbikers, who do much of the trail maintenance. The Tahuya Peninsula is dotted with lakes and ponds; some of the bigger lakes with public fishing access are linked by the State Forest trails.

## LODGINGS

### CADY LAKE MANOR ☆

A most unlikely spot for a lavish bed-and-breakfast with limitless hospitality: off a forest road that wanders over the wild and wooded Tahuya Peninsula. The raison d'être of Cady Lake Manor is Cady Lake, a private 15-acre lake on whose shores Larry De Paul built his brick mansion with the feel of a luxurious fishing lodge. No effort is spared to cod-

### WHERE TO CATCH AN OYSTER

***Public beaches where oysters lie defenseless at low tide abound near and along Hood Canal. Oyster picking is permitted at Potlatch State Park, Lilliwaup, Twanoh State Park, Seal Rock, Dosewallips State Park, and Bywater Bay. Watch for posted warnings and check with the state hotline about the possibility of red tide, when the oysters may be toxic: 800/562-5632. Several oyster farms will shuck the oysters, if you prefer, and sell you bivalves at excellent prices: Hood Canal Seafood (Broad Spit Road, Quilcene; 360/765-3288); Coast Seafoods Company (1570 Linger Longer Road, Quilcene; 360/765-3474); Hama Hama Oyster Company (N 35959 Highway 101, Lilliwaup; 360/877-5811); Taylor Shellfish Farms (130 SE Lynch Road, Shelton; 360/426-6178); and Hunter Farms (E 1921 Highway 106, Union; 360/426-2222).***

dle fishermen and fisherwomen (who account for about half the guests). The lake is stocked with rainbow, cutthroat, and brown trout; fishing is catch-and-release. There's a boat reserved for each guest, and there are also tube boats. Rods may be borrowed. The inn's sumptuously furnished rooms almost overwhelm with displays of antiques and objets d'art. Larry has been a collector as long as he can remember, and one suspects he built such a large inn in order to lodge his treasures. The four spacious bedrooms have queen-size sleigh beds, two have Jacuzzis, and one has a handicapped-accessible sink and shower. Nonfishers may go hiking, mountain biking, golfing (the nearest courses are in Bremerton), or exploring the peninsula and its small towns. But staying right here might be the best bet, there are so many ways to relax. The library has a thousand videos (including many for children), which may be shown on the huge screen. Play pool or cribbage in the game room, sprawl in front of the living-room fireplace, or sit on the deck with its view of the lake nestled in its evergreen forest. Breakfast is included; the four-course dinners are not, but may be reserved. *1471 NE Dewatto Rd, Tahuya; PO Box 2190, Belfair; call for directions; 360/372-2673; $$$; AE, DIS, MC, V; checks OK.* ♿

# HOODSPORT AND THE WESTERN ARM

The largest town on the canal, Hoodsport, strung out along Highway 101, is a good place to stop to investigate hikes into the Olympics, have a meal, taste wine, even spend the night.

## ACTIVITIES

***A Taste of the Grape—and the Berry.*** At Hoodsport Winery, sample the cabernet sauvignon and admire its label, created by painter Amy Burnett of Bremerton. Try the berry and rhubarb wines too, and browse the gift shop, with temptations like raspberry wine and chocolate truffles. Located at N 23501 Highway 101; 360/877-9894. Open daily for tours (see how wine gets from grape or berry to bottle) and for tasting.

***Potlach State Park.*** The west arm of Hood Canal is the jumping-off spot for many recreational areas in the Olympic National Forest and Park, and your direct access to a raft of canalside diversions. Gather your wits and your forces at Potlatch State Park, just south of Hoodsport. It's a handy stop for a picnic or to forage on the beach. At low tide, you have a good chance of gathering oysters, mussels, cockles, butter clams, and littlenecks. There are plenty of shaded trestle tables and benches, and grass is plentiful if you're inclined to set up your deck chair for a snooze.

***Hiking Help.*** Before you head up into the mountains, check at the Hoodsport Ranger Station, just off Highway 101 on Lake Cushman Drive, for campground and hiking information. The single-sheet maps on hand here tell you how steep and difficult the trail is, how long the hike, what flora to watch for, whether there are toilets at the trailhead, and more. Some of the hikes are only a half mile; others are serious backpack trips.

***Lake Cushman.*** This popular lake was created when a wide stretch of the Skokomish River was dammed in the 1920s to provide power for Tacoma, and a 400-acre lake grew to 4,000 acres. The grand old hotels that used to attract the likes of Theodore Roosevelt are long drowned, but modern settlers have built costly summer homes on the shores, and entrepreneurs are filling the hospitality gap. Lake Cushman Resort has cabins, boat rentals, a small grocery, fishing, and swimming (PO Box 148, Hoodsport; 800/588-9630 or 360/877-9630; www.lakecushman.com).

***Hike into the Park.*** At the end of Cushman Lake, the Olympic National Park begins. There's a ranger station, campground, picnicking, and trailheads for a variety of hikes. Even if you didn't bring your hiking boots, take the 2-mile loop along the Staircase Rapids trail, beside the crystal-clear Skokomish; it's a pleasure for both novice and veteran. Many backpack adventures start at Staircase, including the popular Flapjack Lakes trail that rewards with awesome views of the scary-looking Sawtooth Range.

***Two Easy Little Hikes.*** Up the Duckabush River (south of Brinnon) are a couple of good day-hiking trails. The Interrorem Interpretive Trail, a ⅓-mile loop, which begins near the Interrorem Guard Station about 4 miles west of Highway 101, is a cool walk through lush second-growth forest (with plenty of massive stumps to remind you of the first). Connecting to this trail is the equally popular Ranger Hole Trail (1.6 miles round-trip), which leads from the guard station to a stunningly beautiful fishing hole on the Duckabush. Nice picnic grounds near the historic 1907 guard station—a former wilderness outpost—make this a good place to spend an afternoon with the kids.

## LODGINGS

### GLEN AYR RV PARK

In addition to RV parking, Glen Ayr offers 14 handsome large rooms and two suites in its two-story log and knotty-pine motel overlooking the canal. Rooms have TVs and immaculate baths; the decor is muted and soothing. The suites have cooking facilities. And—a rarity in a motel setting—there's a common room for guests: a large, airy space with a big river-stone fireplace, a pool table, card tables, and books and magazines. ("Leave one, take one," says owner Dick Johnson.) Come by boat—Glen Ayr has its

*"People used to come by steamer from Seattle to fish on Lake Cushman and hunt in the area. Guests stayed in tents and the resort had a big dance hall. My family had to row to get their mail and provisions."—A description of Lake Cushman as it was before the dam.*

own moorage. Clamming, crabbing, and oystering are nearby. (Make sure you have your license.) *N25381 Highway 101, Hoodsport; 800/367-9522 or 360/877-9522; $; MC, V; local checks only.*

### MIKE'S BEACH RESORT

Don't expect spiffy at this longtime resort that curves along a cove just before Lilliwaup, north of Hoodsport. Mike Schultz keeps everything chugging right along, and it's as friendly and as close to the water as you can get. Stay in a dorm room or the hostel (these are favored by divers) or bring your RV or tent. Or you could choose one of the well-worn but efficient little cabins on the water, cooking your own food from the resort store (though you'd save a lot by bringing your own). There's so much to do here that many people come back year after year in order to get through the list: dive to examine sunken vessels just offshore; snorkel; go fishing from a rowboat or the dock; launch your own boat for canal cruising; or go kayaking with a kayak rented or purchased from Mike—a short paddle out from the resort is likely to provide views of eagles and seals; loll on the beach; or make this your headquarters for hiking in the Olympic National Forest. *N 38470 Hwy 101, Lilliwaup; 6 miles south of Lilliwaup on Hwy 101; 800/231-5324 or 360/877-5324; mikesbch@hctc.com; $; MC, V; checks OK.*

## BRINNON

Brinnon, hardly more than a wide place in the road, offers access to some of Olympic National Park's best high-country hiking. Situated on Hood Canal between Dosewallips State Park and Seal Rock Campground, Brinnon lies in the shadow of some of the highest peaks in the Olympics—the Brothers, Mount Anderson, and Mount Constance.

## ACTIVITIES

***Dosewallips State Park.*** You'll find convenient rest rooms, picnic and camping sites, and 425 acres of meadows, woodland, and beach at this canal park a mile north of Brinnon, where the "Dose" flows into the canal. Fish for salmon and bottom fish in the canal and for steelhead in the river. The beach has been a favored spot for oystering, clamming, and crabbing, but it's subject to closures; check the state hotline; 800/562-5632.

***Gardens in Bloom.*** From February to June the rhododendrons at Whitney Gardens burst out in a rainbow of colors, at their most blindingly beautiful from late April to mid-May. But a walk through the bushy 6.8-acre maze is delightful anytime, what with magnolias, azaleas, tall evergreens, and maples that are brilliant in fall. Paths are wheelchair-accessible. Plants are available in the nursery, and there's a nice patio area with tables for picnickers. Small admission fee; come any day, but in December and January call ahead. Located at N 31600 Highway 101, Brinnon, WA 98320; 360/796-4411. ♿

***A Good Day Hike.*** From the end of the Dosewallips River Road (15½ miles west of Highway 101), take the West Fork Trail for 2.7 miles to Big Timber Camp, by the river in a stand of Douglas fir and vine maple. The trail goes up and down quite a bit, so you might want to allow a day for the round-trip, with a break for a picnic lunch. Serious hikers go on from Big Timber to backpack right through the Olympics, via Anderson Pass and Enchanted Valley, to Lake Quinault—a 30-mile tramp.

## RESTAURANTS

### HALFWAY HOUSE ★

Everybody seems to know everybody in this small, cozy restaurant, and if you don't when you come in, you will by the time you leave. It makes a convenient break from the drive along the canal, and is one of the few places to eat between Hoodsport and Quilcene. If you're planning to head up the Dosewallips River Road for a hike into the Olympics, very likely someone at the next table can tell you about trail conditions, elk sightings, etc. The rhododendron display at Whitney Gardens is an easy stroll up Highway 101. Best of all, the food's great—check out the homemade soups and pies. Friday is two-for-one steak night; on Saturday, prime rib is the special. Service is quick and friendly. *41 Brinnon Lane, Brinnon; west side of Hwy 101, next to the post* *office; 360/796-4715; $; MC, V; checks OK; full bar; XENALLJ@aol.com.*

## LODGINGS

### ELK MEADOWS BED AND BREAKFAST ☆

View Sleeping in deep comfort right in the middle of an Olympic meadow is pretty close to heaven, and it's what you get at Joy and Joe Baisch's bed and breakfast. Soaring vaulted ceilings, a stunning stone fireplace housing a Russian stove, and not one single Victorian frill, make this place a standout. Decks all around the house and the sunny patios out front lure you to sit watching the woods, the birds, and the azaleas in the Baisches' nursery. Stroll across the meadow to where the Dosewallips flows and watch for an eagle in a treetop. The two rooms may be rented without breakfast, or, for a bit more, with a large country breakfast included; Joy's scones are sublime. Groups sometimes take over the whole inn, and can expand out onto the meadow where they may find themselves sharing RV space with a herd of elk. *3485 Dosewallips Rd, Brinnon; 3½ miles west of Hwy 101 on Dosewallips Rd; 360/796-4886; www.northolympic.com/elkmeadows; elkmeadows@waypt.com; $$; no credit cards; checks OK.*

# QUILCENE

Quilcene, at the north end of Hood Canal, keeps trying to persuade Highway 101 travelers to stop—even going so far as to name a road "Linger Longer." Follow that road to the bay where the Coast Oyster Company (1651 Linger Longer Road; 360/765-3474) sells famous Quilcene oysters at its idyllically situated oyster farm.

## ACTIVITIES

***Oyster Lore.*** At the Point Whitney State Shellfish Laboratory, they'll shell out all the information you can absorb about oysters. Eight miles south of Quilcene, take Bee Mill Road east from 101, and go past Camp Parsons to the lab. Study the interpretive display to learn the mysteries of intertidal life. Then stalk your own wild oyster on the bay side of the nearby sandspit.

It's also a good swimming hole; this is shallow Dabob Bay, where waters are warmer than in the rest of Hood Canal.

***Mount Walker.*** Reached by a 5-mile dirt road (summer only) that winds around the 2,750-foot mountain to the summit, Mount Walker, 5 miles south of Quilcene, offers one of the best views on the peninsula: high peaks of the Olympics to the west, Mounts Baker and Rainier and Glacier Peak to the east, with all of Hood Canal at your feet. Bring a picnic, and come in June to see rhododendrons at their showiest.

***Antiques and More.*** A few miles south of Quilcene, stop at Walker Mountain Trading Post (milepost 300; 360/796-3200). Its couple of rooms are crowded with antiques (mostly local), odd crafts such as a clock that looks like a cow, and jewelry created by local artists. You may also pick up smoked salmon, fresh oysters, ice cream bars, and pop.

***At the south end of Quilcene, get acquainted with sociable locals at the Whistling Oyster Tavern, which has been there just about forever; 360/765-9508.***

## RESTAURANTS

### TIMBER HOUSE

Surrounded by cedar and hemlock, the Timber House resembles nothing so much as a hunting lodge gussied up to make it comfortable for the womenfolk. Descriptive logging scenes are painted on the hand-carved tables and counter-ledges: a nice touch. The local seafood is the main reason to eat here. Quilcene oysters come from down the road, and there's much more from the waters around the Sound. Dungeness crab is a winner: sautéed, as a sandwich filling, in an omelet, or a salad. Locals swear by the roast-beef dinners. Monday is Mexican night. *PO Box 545; about ½ mile south of Quilcene on Hwy 101; 360/765-3339; $$; MC, V; checks OK; lunch, dinner Thurs–Mon; full bar.* ♿

### TWANA ROADHOUSE

This modest establishment offers good simple meals with no fuss. That must be what its public wants, because the roadhouse is expanding into the defunct Twana Trading Post next door. Eat in a cheerful room where tourists and locals mingle. The menu won't dazzle, but everything is fresh: soups, salads, sandwiches, pizzas, plus homemade pies and hand-dipped ice cream. *29473 Hwy 101, Quilcene; east side of Hwy 101 at south end of town; 360/765-6485; $; MC,V; checks OK; breakfast, lunch, and dinner every day; no alcohol; twanaroadhouse@hotmail.com.* ♿

# INDEX

## A



## B



## C

## D



## E



## F



## G

## P



## Q



## R



## S

## T



## U



## V



## W

BEST PLACES®

**DESTINATIONS**

# OLYMPIC PENINSULA

## REPORT FORM

*Based on my personal experience, I wish to nominate the following restaurant or place of lodging; or confirm/correct/disagree with the current review.*

*(Please include address and telephone number of establishment, if convenient.)*

## REPORT

*Please describe food, service, style, comfort, value, date of visit, and other aspects of your experience; continue on another piece of paper if necessary.*

*I am not concerned, directly or indirectly, with the management or ownership of this establishment.*

SIGNED

ADDRESS

PHONE DATE

*Please address to Best Places Destinations and send to:*

SASQUATCH BOOKS
615 Second Avenue, Suite 260
Seattle, WA 98104
Feel free to email feedback as well: books@sasquatchbooks.com